TWILIGHT
OF THE
IDOLS:

An American Story

Cover design by K.F. Creative Consulting
Interior by Bryan Tomasovich at The Publishing World

Olson, Brayden W.B.
Twilight of the Idols: An American Story

1. Political Science—Political Economy. 2. Political Science—Public Policy /
Economic Policy. 3. Political Ideologies—General.

Printed in the U.S.A.

TWILIGHT
OF THE
IDOLS:

An American Story

Brayden W.B. Olson

For my grandmother, who with her life showed me how to...

speak with kindness, even with whom you disagree, so that you might be able to truly hear them;

see the lessons of her time, now present again in mine;

walk softly on this earth;

love unconditionally;

and how, in these ways, to be of service to my family, community, country, and world.

Foreword

As a Representative of the people, I have spent countless hours talking with individuals and groups: going door-to-door, sitting in meetings, talking on the phone, and answering questions in the grocery store aisle. In my role as State Representative it is my responsibility to be the voice of my district, and to do so, I spend a lot of time conversing with the people of my district and state.

What I have learned from these conversations is that we have different upbringings and professions. We have each faced our own share of challenges and unique obstacles. We have also been influenced differently by culture, from our heritage and nationality to our education and the media. Yet, despite this, we are all more similar to each other than we are different. Yes, even in these times we have more in common with our neighbor or a stranger than we differ from them.

Brayden and I sit on different sides of the political aisle, and like so many of us it takes just a few conversations to realize how much more we all have in common as Americans than that which divides us.

This may seem like an easy concept to grasp; however, if you survey our political landscape you see polarization and stagnation. People are divided into differing camps with seemingly little, to nothing in common. I have learned that I am a better Representative when I listen to differing points of view. I believe strongly that the path to problem solving and solutions for our states and country is one where we listen to one another, finding appreciation for our similarities, and strength in our differences.

Regardless of where a person falls on the political spectrum, it is evident that challenges are surmounting around us. As a country, we are in a new place where higher levels of debt, a diminishing middle class, and new automation threatens our economic structure. Our old solutions won't fix these new problems. Instead, we must begin to ask new questions: How do we ensure liberty and justice is truly available to all? How do we build an economy that gives a path for hardworking people today to get out of student debt, buy a home, and save for retirement? Asking more questions will lead to new answers and new opportunities for growth and prosperity for people.

As an innovator and entrepreneur, Brayden Olson is accustomed to challenging the status quo—questioning convention to improve upon it and creating new solutions. In business and education, Brayden has asked, *How can companies find their future talent?* And, *How can students be better prepared for success after college?* His answer is through gaming technology. In politics, Brayden has asked, *What can we do to improve the position of our great country and its people?* His answer: writing this book so we can start acknowledging what is changing around us. Our country is always changing, and so too must our thinking.

This book is meant to be an easily accessible window into the various challenges that are today challenging our concept of the American Dream. It's meant to invoke questions and discussion. It's meant to make these large political concepts accessible to those outside of politics. Finally, it's meant to inspire people to take action within their own lives and communities. Change comes through acknowledging the problems around us and setting our eyes on the solutions we want.

We need people who are willing to put party label aside, political ideology on the backburner, and business and lobby interests behind the unwavering focus on increasing the success of people. To stay true to our founding and be a government for and by the people, we must be willing to look at where our country has been, where we currently are, and ask how we can advance to a more prosperous future. This book will take you on that journey. The answers to our challenges will come when we start asking the new questions. I invite you to begin asking new questions.

—Representative Melanie Stambaugh
  25th District, Washington State Legislature

Introduction

"The only thing necessary for the triumph of evil is that good men should do nothing."

—Edmund Burke (attributed)
   as referenced by President John F. Kennedy

Why is the current, emerging generation the first in American history projected to be economically worse off than our parents?

What is the root cause of our systematic decline?

What is our best chance of doing something about it?

If you're like me, these are the questions that keep you up at night.

This book isn't written to sell copies. It isn't being written to support the political agenda of Republicans or Democrats. It's not supporting a campaign. Instead, it's intended to address these questions that we need to talk about now, at a defining moment in United States history.

If you take away nothing else from this book, know that the point is this: spiraling economic inequality is at the root of virtually every other major issue we are concerned about today.

Twilight of the Idols

I understand you may be coming into this book with a wildly different perspective and want evidence to validate such a claim. While this Introduction is not the place for those details, I can promise you that each chapter of this book will provide a new layer into the details you seek.

You might even be of the opinion that economic inequality is a key driver of the American Dream. To some extent, it is. Having an appropriate incentive is key to motivating innovation and entrepreneurship.

I'm talking about something different. A kind of economic inequality that is getting further and further outside of the norm we saw during our periods of greatest economic growth. A kind of economic inequality that is making it nearly impossible for hardworking people to live without debt, which is why more than 70 percent of Americans will now die in debt.[1]

Whether you are concerned about housing, education, health care, immigration, environmental policy, the prison system, or even the opioid epidemic, the root cause is the same. Our country is faltering in its tracks, and pushing people to their breaking points because of economic inequality. This isn't about some people having a lot more and others a lot less. It's about having systems in place that ensure hardworking Americans fall further behind and that the wealthy need not work at all to watch their wealth continue to skyrocket. It's become a rigged game. A game we see being played out in dramatic extremes. In more than a century, we've only seen the kind of wealth inequality we are seeing today during the time of the Great Depression.[2] The top .1 percent now own well over 20 percent of US wealth, the highest level we've seen since before the Great Depression. [3]

---

1 Jennifer Calfas, "Americans Have So Much Debt They're Taking It to The Grave," *Money*, last modified March 22, 2017. http://time.com/money/4709270/americans-die-in-debt.

2 Emmanuel Saez and Gabriel Zucman, "Exploding Wealth Inequality in the United States," Washington Center for Equitable Growth, last modified October 20, 2014. https://equitablegrowth.org/exploding-wealth-inequality-united-states.

3 Saez and Zucman, "Exploding Wealth Inequality in the United States."

Brayden W.B. Olson

You may be reading this and thinking, *Economic inequality isn't nearly as important as smaller government, environment, or (insert your issue here).* To you I say, read on, because you will find that virtually every issue you might care about is being caused or exaggerated by economic inequality.

Or, you might be thinking, *economic inequality is the engine of capitalism and a good thing.* To you I say, yes, but only within reason. If you want to preserve entrepreneurship, innovation, and market competition, read on, because the backbone of our capitalist economy is at stake.

As I said, the game is rigged, but let me put this another way. It *is* provable—statistically, and based on the clearest of evidences—that it is now more difficult for hardworking people to get ahead than it was just ten years ago. And, it is far more difficult than it was twenty years ago. Average median household income in 1996 was about $54,000.[4] In 2016, it was about $59,000. Yet, median housing costs rose from $132,000 in January 1996 to $288,000 in January 2016, or from 2.4x annual household wages to 4.9x annual household wages.[5] Out of state tuition for public universities rose 157 percent.[6] In-state tuition for public universities rose 237 percent. From housing, education, food, gas, and clothing, life really has become more expensive. And, it's been getting steadily worse since the 1980s.

In most cases, American people are working harder than ever, but they're not getting ahead. The American Dream is disappearing before our eyes and on our watch. Since the turn of the century,

---

4   "Average (median) Household Income in the United States from 1990 to 2017 (in U.S. dollars)," Statista, accessed November 26, 2018, https://www.statista.com/statistics/200838/median-household-income-in-the-united-states/.

5   "Median and Average Sale Price of Houses Sold in the United States," United States Census Bureau, accessed November 26, 2018, https://www.census.gov/construction/nrs/pdf/uspricemon.pdf.

6   Briana Boyington, "See 20 Years of Tuition Growth at National Universities," *U.S. News & World Report*, accessed November 26, 2018, https://www.usnews.com/education/best-colleges/paying-for-college/articles/2017-09-20/see-20-years-of-tuition-growth-at-national-universities.

we've watched poverty in this country skyrocket. While it changes from year-to-year, which is often used to downplay the trend, it's higher today and impacting far more people than it was at the end of the last century.[7] This extends far beyond the Great Recession.

This is a key distinction. There are those who see this kind of talk and say it focuses on blame rather than solutions. Whining rather than finding a way.

It's quite the opposite. At a minimum, we are talking about providing the same opportunity to *pick yourself up and succeed* that used to exist. It's that simple; reset the game rules to allow the same hardworking people to succeed to the same extent as they used to.

There are solutions, and we can execute them, but not in a state of delusion. This book encourages all Americans to embrace the reality of our current situation so that we may then address the solutions. In short, the first step to solving a problem is admitting that there is one, and this book will walk the reader through exploring some commonly held beliefs that are no longer valid. In the book's title, I call them *idols*, because these greatly revered ideas no longer truly exist. They have passed away in our short lifetimes.

Listening to all of this, wondering whether I'm right, you'll want to know who I am to be able to speak on these issues, and that's more than fair. So, am I an economist? A scholar? A politician? A businessman or a job creator? The answer is that I'm a concerned young American who has been sitting in all of these circles, but not fully in just one of them. And it's precisely this perspective that has helped me put the puzzle pieces together.

You see, because of the background I came from, I couldn't just shake these questions of inequality. I've known what it is to fear buying food for the sake of an overdraft charge. And, before I got the scholarship I needed to afford my education, I remember having to justify to myself why it would be okay if I never went to

---

7 "Poverty rate in the United States from 1990 to 2017," Statista, accessed November 26, 2018, https://www.statista.com/statistics/200463/us-poverty-rate-since-1990/.

school. Knowing in my heart that it is getting harder every year, I look over my shoulder knowing that had I been born just a few years later, I wouldn't have an education or run my own business. Every year, fewer kids have any chance at all at the American Dream.

*

My name is Brayden Olson, and like many of you, I grew up in a middle-class family. In my case, it was a struggling middle-class family. As a result, I saw the adversity faced by anyone who wanted to *make it*. And, yes, the adversity pushed me forward—but that's not always enough, and so I'll say here and now that I got lucky in a lot of ways. I got my education, graduating *Magna Cum Laude* and *Beta Gamma Sigma* eighteen months after graduating high school. I became a self-made entrepreneur and business owner who knows the challenges of signing the front side of a check to create jobs. I was selected as one of five "Startup Idols" by *Fortune*, Young Professional of the Year by my city, and the youngest entrepreneur admitted to Seattle's Entrepreneurs' Organization. I'm also an inventor whose patent pending technology is helping advance education, and I received a National Science Foundation grant to support that work. I've also worked on successful economic legislation, held a legislative action position, and run for public political office. And that run led me inexorably to write this book.

I wasn't born into it. So, there isn't a second that goes by where I forget that I was a hair's breadth from none of it ever happening, no matter how hard I worked. If I had been born just a few years later, I would have had to give up to survive. My situation was so fragile that if my tuition has been just $1,000 more than it was, none of the above would have happened.

I overloaded my classes, went to school in the summer, worked in the school cafeteria, and launched my business all at the same time. If it had taken me one month longer to get funding for my business, or I had been forced to give up one month sooner, I wouldn't be a business owner. That's why my heart goes out to the kids coming up now who, just like me, have the will, but, unlike me, won't have the way.

The American people can't be saved by politicians and researchers. It's going to take the people speaking up who see the system as a whole. You reading this book is another step in that direction.

In the coming chapters, I'll explain what is happening and how it is happening. I'll lay things out and go through the details, which is precisely where the economists, academics, and politicians have been falling short. Part of the problem is that our leaders continue to stress ideas, through popular talking points, that haven't been true for quite some time: like America being the land of opportunity, and all that separates you from wealth is hard work. They earn a cheap and easy clap, but these words are as hollow as the idols they now represent.

That's why I chose the title *Twilight of the Idols: An American Story*. One hundred and fifty years ago, Friedrich Nietzsche wrote the original *Twilight of the Idols* to discuss cultural shifts underway during what he described as an, "epoch of political decline." It is that spirit of choosing to critique the dominant culture of the time, not the contents therein from a long time ago, that led to this title. To discuss the ideas and deeply held beliefs that today feel as if they are beyond reproach, change, or action but need more than anything to be torn down. Further, to recognize the values, ideas, and beliefs so deeply rooted in the American Dream that we see them as unchangeable, but which are today already in transition or completely gone from our culture.

I also benefited greatly from the in-depth economic research of Thomas Piketty, whom I will reference many times throughout this book.

As we explore these idols—ranging from being the land of opportunity to being a government of the people, for the people— I'll also explain how, with each year that passes, the American people—and, frankly, even our representatives in Washington—have less and less of a voice in the decision-making process, which is one of the reasons we need to change things now, if we still can. Partisanship is divisive, and it's also a distraction that's taking us away from focusing on what matters and how we can fix it. We have far more in common with each other than any differences we have.

In fact, I have no doubt both sides of the aisle are trying to do good in this world in the best way they know how. It's a difference of perspective rather than intent. A friend and mentor once told me, "Conservative-oriented people often find their truth intrinsically turning to family, tradition, experience, or religion. Liberally-oriented people often find their truth externally by turning to research, experts, and statistics. Neither is right and both have their flaws." Once I embraced that idea, it became so much easier to understand and listen to the ideas every side brought to the table. After all, we can only learn when we listen, and the less information we have the worse our decisions will be.

Finally, after you have a chance to see past all of the myths and understand the evidence that proves economic inequality is at the heart of our country's problems, I'll share specifically what we can do about it. And I'm not talking about abstract goals or superfluous ones. I'm talking about sharing with you the exact steps that you, and we, as American citizens, can take—immediately.

The fact is that there is a credible path in front of us that could lead to taking our country back as early as 2020: a constitutional convention. This convention, also known as a Convention of States, could impose strict term limits on our congressional representatives, severely restrict the amount of money spent on political campaigns, and create a new system to enforce government ethics.

I'll explain a lot more about this later, but for now, know that a movement is already underway in twenty-eight states, and it has millions of followers behind it. We just need seven more states to become involved, and as long as we make the goals of this campaign understood, that shouldn't be difficult. Polls have consistently shown that nearly all American people want to see campaign finance reform and term limits—in fact, there are almost no topics in our country that are more unilaterally supported by the people.[8][9][10] If you put these reforms to a popular vote for ratification, as the Convention of States could, then the American people will be able to rise up with one united voice to demand them. Believe it or not (and I understand that, right now, you might be skeptical), these changes are not out of reach.

The Convention of States movement brings these changes tantalizingly close. The simple changes of campaign finance reform and term limits can transform our government and weaken the political establishment so we can reclaim Lincoln's vision of a government of the people, by the people, and for the people.

It's an opportunity, not a silver bullet. It will still require massive civic involvement by the people in this country. Like Civil Rights or Women's Liberation was for prior generations, reclaiming a government for the people will have to become the civic movement of my generation if we are to succeed--and that is the key to the economic equality that will give the generation behind us a chance at the Dream.

---

8   John McLaughlin and Brittany Davin, "M&A Poll: Voters Overwhelmingly Support Term Limits for Congress," McLaughlin & Associates, accessed November 26, 2018, http://mclaughlinonline.com/2018/02/08/ma-poll-voters-overwhelmingly-support-term-limits-for-congress/.

9   Katie Glueck, "Poll: 75 Percent Want Hill Term Limits," *The Politico*, last modified January 18, 2013, https://www.politico.com/story/2013/01/poll-75-percent-want-hill-term-limits-086378.

10   Drew Desilver and Patrick Van Kessel, "As More Money Flows into Campaigns, Americans Worry about Its Influence," Pew Research Center, last modified December 7, 2015, http://www.pewresearch.org/fact-tank/2015/12/07/as-more-money-flows-into-campaigns-americans-worry-about-its-influence/.

Chapter 1

Whatever Happened to the Land of Opportunity?

"First they came for the Socialists, and I did not speak out—
Because I was not a Socialist.

Then they came for the Trade Unionists, and I did not speak out—
Because I was not a Trade Unionist.

Then they came for the Jews, and I did not speak out—
Because I was not a Jew.

Then they came for me—and there was no one left to speak for
me."

—Martin Niemöller

"In fact, statistics show not only that our levels of income
inequality rank near countries like Jamaica and Argentina, but
that it is harder today for a child born here in America to improve
her station in life than it is for children in most of our wealthy
allies, countries like Canada or Germany or France. They have
greater mobility than we do."

—Barack Obama, December 4, 2013[11]

11   Mark Thoma, "Remarks by the President on Economic Mobility," *Economist's View*, last modified December 4, 2013, https://economistsview.typepad.com/economistsview/2013/12/remarks-by-the-president-on-economic-mobility.html.

From its founding, the United States has endeavored to be a nation of promise and opportunity, to be a people not demeaned by monarch, caste, or class, who have the freedom to follow their own dreams and beliefs. These goals of our country were focused on the need to find freedom, and on equality; although those may be lofty ideals, they have been the cornerstones of not just our founding, but our progress and our success. The struggles our nation went through for independence, and the growth that has followed ever since, have all been rooted in the belief that we as a nation have the ability to not just promise opportunity and success, but actually meet our goals in a way that allows for the success of our nation as a whole. Our path forward has ever been focused on promise, opportunity, freedom, and equality, both as a nation and as individuals.

Of course, there's no question that our country has stumbled and fallen short on these promises at different times, and for different groups of people. We can't ignore that, either.

We were a nation that embraced slavery, and that fight brought us to civil war. Servitude was only fully eradicated a century later as the result of the Civil Rights revolution that ended the segregation laws known as Jim Crow laws, and we still have a long distance to go before we'll be completely out of the shadow of the terrible prejudices. Not many people know that the state constitutions of Vermont and Oregon once forbade residence for U.S. citizens of African descent, which itself suggests just how far we've come. Likewise, our nation needed to draft, debate, and pass an amendment to its Constitution in order to enfranchise women. And along the way, there have been any number of groups who have faced prejudice and even violence because of their heritage, their beliefs, or their way of life. We're not beyond these struggles, though we're making progress.

Notably, though, for each of these moments, each of these struggles, there have been great women and men who have come forward to remind us of our ideals, and to fight for those Americans who were suffering—and these individuals are as much a part of our history as anything else. Some are still fighting, and many others are remembered for embodying our highest American ideals. In many cases, they have stepped forward to remind us, in part, that some moments in history demand larger participation in a government like ours, where our people stand up as a single, multi-volumed voice and demand change, reminding every citizen of those promises for opportunity.

There are no perfect heroes in our history, or any history. As humans, they too struggled to live by those greater ideals, but for them success meant eventually creating a society where everyone had a chance to succeed. This was not formed by those select few leaders we remember today. It was not just Jefferson, Lincoln, Kennedy, King and the handful of other names that are part of our cultural zeitgeist. It was built by the countless people whose names we may not know today, but who believed in these ideals. By lesser know names, like Ralph Emerson and Henry Thoreau, who published and supported ideas of civil disobedience should a state become unjust. A tradition carried on today by those like Edward Snowden who, whether you agree or disagree with his methods, has pushed us to ask questions about what we want the future of our country to be and which values we prioritize more highly.

We built a country where people are in control of their government, not the other way around, and where every child has an opportunity to improve their social and economic station. My concern is that after all that struggle, and all those sacrifices, these ideals are being lost right before our eyes, in our time.

You see, any nation worthy of greatness must always be in a state of continual reform and expansion of its promise. Growth comes from struggle, and from change, and in order for our nation to follow through on its ideals on behalf of its people, we must continuously remember to invest in and pursue our ideals. That means embracing change, and on occasion risk, because a great nation that exists in a changing world must itself be willing to change. And that's fine—we just have to keep going. Fall down six times, and then get up seven.

Twilight of the Idols

Since the end of the Second World War, the United States has emerged as an undisputed world leader and extended a promise of sorts to the entire world. For many decades, that promise and the meaning behind it, embodied by the freedom and perseverance of our nation's people, was very clear. However, today, we find ourselves in a very different position, and it's not a comfortable one. The whole world is watching us struggle, even as we try to understand how things began coming apart as they have, and that's why you're reading this book.

In the Post-War years, economic equality hit an all time high. Prior to WWII, the top 1 percent in the United States owned 23.9 percent of the total income of the country.[12] In the years that followed, we saw a sharp decline from the 1930s through the start of the 1980s, where that number dropped to 8.9 percent. During that time, economic mobility entered its peak.

As previously mentioned, we've watched American life become increasingly difficult. In the last twenty years, median household income has barely changed, but the average cost of a house has more than doubled. Tuition doubled and tripled. Across the board, housing, education, food, gas, clothing, and all of life's necessities started eating up more and more of our total income.

As such, we've taken the only option available to us: take on debt. A supermajority of Americans will now live and die in debt.[13] And that debt eliminates our economic mobility. It removes the ability to take risks like starting a company. Student debt has become the primary reason Millennials aren't starting companies like prior generations.[14] It also prevents the ability to save, invest, and diversify. If your only source of income is your salary, and 105

---

12   Emmanuel Saez, "Striking it Richer: The Evolution of Top Incomes in the United States (Updated with 2015 preliminary estimates)," Econometrics Laboratory at the University of California at Berkeley, last modified June 30, 2016, https://eml.berkeley.edu/~saez/saez-UStopincomes-2015.pdf.

13   Jennifer Calfas, "Americans Have So Much Debt They're Taking It to The Grave."

14   Derek Thompson, "The Myth of the Millennial Entrepreneur," The Atlantic, last modified July 6, 2016, https://www.theatlantic.com/business/archive/2016/07/the-myth-of-the-millennial-entrepreneur/490058/.

percent of your salary is taken by the cost of living and your debt payments, then how will we as a nation ever get ahead?

In the nineteenth century, indentured servitude was a contract you signed to commit yourself to years of labor, under which you had no freedom to pursue other options. You could not marry without the permission of your master, nor did you have many other rights. You were the property of your employer until you had served your time. The 13th Amendment abolished this practice in 1865. Yet today, in the twenty-first century, the choices we are making in Congress are institutionalizing debt into the middle class. It's becoming a way of life that is radically reducing the choices Americans have over their own lives. Our youngest generation is pushing off marriage, because they can't afford it or stabilize their lives, and fewer among them are becoming homeowners than in recorded history. Sure, they can change employers, but the fact that a vast majority of the people in our country will live and die with a lifetime of debt, no matter the choices they make, has an eerie similarity to systems we have long since tried to eliminate.

We stand at a precipice. Do we let economic mobility decline in this country? If not, then we must pursue economic policies that reward hard work, not wealth. Policies that truly give the middle class choice and the ability to chart a path toward mobility.

Now we need to take a hard look at one of those myths I mentioned earlier. Is the United States still the land of opportunity? If you work hard in this country, can that alone provide the fundamental needs for you and your family?

The promise and the opportunity of the United States was never about avoiding hard work or being unwilling to apply oneself and get something done. It was about providing ever-growing numbers of its citizens with the ability to pursue happiness and freedom. That meant that citizens had to work for their happiness and freedom, but there was always a clear road forward to reaching those ever-present goals. If you worked hard, there was a way to provide all the fundamental needs for your family—from food to education.

Twilight of the Idols

We approached the precipice mentioned above starting around 1980, when, for the first time since we've had statistics to measure the economy, productivity and efficiency increased, but wages stagnated. Measurements captured by the Economic Policy Institution show productivity and wages growing steadily together until about 1973. [15] By the 1980s we see productivity skyrocket and compensation get completely left behind—we were working harder, getting more done, and seeing massive increases in profit for business owners, but regular Americans were no longer participating in that growth. As individual Americans, we weren't able to save more money, increase the quality of our lives, have a bigger Christmas celebration for the kids, or anything else we might have been dreaming about. We were working harder, but with the goal of maintaining our status quo rather than improving it. And at some point, maintaining the status quo became not just a little bit of extra work, but a struggle. For many Americans, the dream went from a bigger house and being able to afford to send your kids to the best university they can achieve to struggling to hold onto the house you've got and co-signing massive loans for your kids to afford even the least expensive option they have.

Like many people, I grew up in a family where my parents struggled financially to survive. Sometimes holding down as many as three jobs, my parents worked hard just to make ends meet. Growing up, there were no rainy-day funds, family vacations, special outings to celebrate birthdays, and no savings—for college or anything else. We lived knowing that one emergency, accident, or serious medical issue would wreck us. It was the struggle of Sisyphus, who constantly pushed a boulder to the top of a hill each day, only to have it roll down to the bottom by the next morning. As a kid, this was the norm I grew up with.

This isn't an easy existence. And no matter how hard you're working, as an adult, there's a lot of stress involved. It's not easy to have to tell your kids that you don't get paid for a few more days,

---

15 "The Productivity–Pay Gap," Economic Policy Institute, last modified August 2018, https://www.epi.org/productivity-pay-gap/.

so a trip to the grocery store or that new movie is going to have to wait. And as a kid, it's not easy to ask for something you need for school, which your teacher says you have to get, even when you know your parents really can't afford it.

For me, as a kid, I didn't know the details, but I knew I didn't see my mom and dad as often as I should (because they were working), and I felt guilty for wanting anything that was remotely expensive. I knew it wasn't normal that my brother would bring home leftover pizza from the pizza shop he worked at so that I could have dinner at eleven o'clock at night. I remember picking up second-hand clothes, and later in life telling my parents I didn't want to go to college because I didn't see how I could work my way out of the debt. And I knew my parents argued over money. But, I also knew they were working like crazy to provide a good life for us.

The truth is, our national character stresses self-reliance, and sometimes this leads us to thumb our noses at folks who were born with disadvantages we couldn't possibly understand. After all, we can't all be above average, can we? The bootstrap mentality can be a harsh judge. For some, their struggles really can be overcome with hard work. Unfortunately, in many cases people with these solvable disadvantages then go on to assume that all anyone needs to succeed is a bit more hard work.

Even for those who understand that isn't true, and are empathetic to systemic oppression, it's a lot easier to think that hard work can solve anything, than to think that some people are truly stuck in suffering, and that there's nothing you can do to help them. Because, realistically, you're in a position where you probably do have to put yourself and your family first, for fear that you'll be the ones who desperately need help tomorrow.

Sometimes we lock ourselves in the cellar of despair, blaming ourselves if we suffer misfortune, without asking questions about the larger social and economic systems in which we're all enmeshed. We keep quiet about our struggles because we feel we have nothing and no one to blame but ourselves. Mass media project rosy images where everyone else seems to be doing so well. If all of those families on television and in commercials can make things work so easily, why shouldn't you be able to? It seems like it has to be your fault. If you just try hard enough, you'll succeed. If you haven't succeeded, it means you haven't tried hard enough. A sense of shame and isolation keeps us from speaking out, but I'm here to tell you that you're not alone and that it's not your fault.

You didn't choose to be born at a time when the cost of a house and an education is more than twice as much of your income as it was twenty years ago. No matter how hard you work, it won't change those facts. Nor does it change the fact that if you worked fewer hours twenty years ago, you'd still be economically much better off.

In today's social media era where you compare your real life to everyone else's "highlight reel," this isolation can become unbearable. In my own life experience, during some of the darkest moments of my life, I've been absolutely dumbfounded by how even my closest friends perceived my life to be successful. At such times, I was starting my first business having little more than a glorified storage closet for an office and was struggling to afford food. I've also seen one of my most admired friends who seemed to have it all—beauty, brains, health, success, and a clear, meaningful purpose in life—struggle with hopelessness, depression and suicide. We all feel alone. We all feel like the only one with the problem. If only we could better pierce each other's solitude so much of this pain would go away.

So, before we dig into the details, let's talk about the situations almost all of us find ourselves in right now:

For whatever reason, you are or were unable to afford a college education. In this situation, you're experiencing the greatest wage gap in recorded history for those without a college degree.[16] In the past, this had far less impact on your ability to make a living,

---

16   Christopher S. Rugaber, "Pay Gap between College Grads and Everyone Else at a Record," *USA Today*, last modified January 12, 2017, https://www.usatoday. com/story/money/2017/01/12/pay-gap-between-college-grads-and-everyone-else-record/96493348/.

but today the wages on these jobs make savings impossible and debts likely. This is likely to most heavily apply to Millennials and Generation Xers living now.

Or, you did get a college education in the last fifteen years, and are more heavily burdened with college debt than at any point in recorded history. It's now over $1.4 trillion, by the way.[17] You make more income than your non-degreed fellow Americans, but you're struggling with debt and interest payments that may only be rivaled by your rent. Unless, like more than at any other time in American history, you've had to move back home. In which case, this debt is your greatest expense. In either case, your financial independence may be decades away. This is likely to most heavily apply to Millennials.

You've actually become a homeowner, but are realizing it is harder than it used to be to make ends meet given that the cost of mortgages is now a much larger chunk of your income than it used to be. While you're in a better position than many, you probably have little to no idea how you'll be able to pay your children's college tuition when the time comes or save for any meaningful retirement. In this camp, you're likely to be a Gen Xer or Boomer.

You're someone who experienced economic growth and savings, made investments, and invested in homes. You've either just barely recovered from 2008, or haven't. Your family probably needs your help and you also know your best income years are behind you. In fact, another disaster and you might need the help. If you've had an economic setback either recently or earlier in life, you might also be experiencing a great deal of uncertainty about maintaining any reasonable quality of life with little hope of being able to change that in the future. This may speak to some Gen Xers, but predominantly will be Boomers.

Everyone alive today is being impacted, but we're being impacted in different ways. So, what is happening here?

---

17 "A Look at the Shocking Student Loan Debt Statistics for 2018," Student Loan Hero, last modified May 1, 2018, https://studentloanhero.com/student-loan-debt-statistics/.

Twilight of the Idols

From the beginning of the higher education boom that began with the GI Bill following World War II, and on until the late '80s, most people had an affordable way to finance college, allowing them to be full-time students and also emerge with a degree with almost no debt. Partially, this access to education was due to the fact that community colleges and state universities once had negligible tuitions, if any tuition at all, and scholarships and grants were available for books and housing. Put simply, getting a college degree actually didn't cost all that much money. Not relative to what it costs now.

Now, students and their parents are asked to take on enormous debt. Loans are plentiful, but they're a trap for building debt that will follow students for decades after they graduate. Scholarships can be godsends, but they often cover only partial costs—at best, they tend to cover tuition while students still have to find a way to pay for room and board, books and supplies, and any other expenses. Additionally, for thirty-five years, college costs have been increasing faster than everything else in our society, except health care. There's the giant expense of tuition, but after that, there are a multitude of other expenses to be accounted for: meal plans, housing, textbooks, and much more. It's not uncommon for a single textbook to cost hundreds of dollars, and that's one textbook for one class, when the average student will take at least four classes per semester. All of a sudden, we're seeing students who have scholarships to help them pay for school, and still they're taking on extra jobs, and either credit cards or student loans, just to make sure they can get that all-important degree. The scholarship is something, but it's not nearly enough. And that's assuming you even have one.

For a while, it didn't require working outside of school for most people to pay for their education. Then, for a time, a little hard work could get you through without any debt. But today, no matter how hard you work today, you simply can't deliver 120 hours' worth of pizzas in a week to pay for that full-time education. Thus, you're faced with either decades of struggle with debt, or a lifetime of struggles with wages.

If you did choose debt, chances are you're paying the equivalent of your first mortgage just to stay above water on your student loans, with no appreciating real estate asset to show for it. A debt that is making a lot of life's decisions for you from the inability to own a home, start a family or start a business. It's hard to know which scenario is more difficult.

Our capitalist economy has always had its ups and downs, booms and busts. But, across the 19th century until the end of the 1970s, you couldn't find a decade period where the average American wages didn't increase.[18] That's one major reason the U.S. has been a magnet for immigrants during most of its history—our nation constantly delivered on that promise of opportunity. But, since the 1980s, the wins were no longer shared with American workers, but the failures were paid for by them. Even more troubling, net worth shows us diverging into a huge group of "have-nots" and a tiny sliver of "have-yachts." It's not education that matters so much anymore, but the resources your family had. That's not my America. And, if you're alive today, you're probably becoming more and more painfully aware of the acceleration of wealth to fewer hands. At the height of the 1 percent movement, 388 people held the same wealth as the bottom 3.5 billion people in the world. By 2017, it was just 8.[19]

Since the New Deal eighty years ago, it's been a federal, state, and local priority to encourage homeownership. We made it as accessible to everyone as possible, because we knew homeownership was one of the surest ways to create equity, savings, and security for the middle class. Plus, you could deduct the interest of your mortgage from your taxable income, which amounted to the largest version of middle-class "wealthfare" in human history.

---

18   Richard Wolff, "The Myth of 'American Exceptionalism' Implodes," *The Guardian,* last modified January 18, 2011, https://www.theguardian.com/commentisfree/cifamerica/2011/jan/17/economics-globalrecession.

19   Deborah Hardoon, "An Economy for the 99%: It's time to build a human economy that benefits everyone, not just the privileged few," Oxfam, last modified January 16, 2017, https://policy-practice.oxfam.org.uk/publications/an-economy-for-the-99-its-time-to-build-a-human-economy-that-benefits-everyone-620170.

Twilight of the Idols

Today, despite the occasional hype about how well Millennial homeownership is going, we've reached the low point for at least any of the living generations. We have more young people living at home than at any point in recorded U.S. history. China, on the other hand, has *double* the rates of homeownership in its Millennial population, at 70 percent. And Mexico also leads us in Millennial homeownership by double digits.[20]

You might wonder why it matters how another country is doing when it comes to this particular statistic. Simply, homeownership rates today are the strength of the middle class today and tomorrow. It foreshadows what is to come. And, presently, the young adults in our country are falling behind countries both competitive and allied that we would have never imagined would have a stronger middle class than we do.

Without the ability to grow equity in a home or to save in more traditional ways, given higher expenses and lower incomes, we have built a world of economic precarity.

Rather than a land of opportunity we have formed a new social class: *the precariat*. Debt and anxiety are the new normal—and they're constant.

Today, 73 percent of Americans die in debt—$61,554 in debt, on average[21]—and virtually every metric indicates that things are likely to only become harder for your children. That twenty-first century form of indentured servitude I discussed before—it is life in this precariat. There are no more chains, but there are two classes: the working poor, and the wealthy who need not work.

In fact, *The Washington Post* recently published a piece discussing the bestselling 2014 book, *Capital in the Twenty-First Century,* written by the researcher I referenced in the Introduction, Thomas Piketty, in which data reveal that, all told, you're likely to become wealthier from having wealth and not working than from

20   Taylor Tepper, "Millennials in China are Twice as Likely to Own Homes as Young Americans," *Money,* last modified April 10, 2017, http://time.com/money/4732889/millennials-home-ownership-china-america/.

21   Jennifer Calfas, "Americans Have So Much Debt They're Taking It to The Grave."

participating in the working economy.[22] For the wealthiest among us, we've virtually eliminated risk. Similarly captured in *Capital in the Twenty-First Century* is the fact that the larger the fortune, the more it consists of primarily financial assets (think "paperwealth" like stocks and partnerships). Yet, when the U.S. government and U.S. Federal Reserve bailed out the banks in 2008, $3.5 trillion went to these financial assets while just $831 billion was intended to help the general public.[23]

If you have enough wealth, you can speculate on financial assets and win big. If you lose, the government will bail you out. On the other hand, if your life is tied into a hard asset, like a home, well just two years after 2008, 1.2 million Americans had lost their homes.[24]

We've gotten to a point where many of you probably expected to read what I just shared. It's not surprising to you at all. But, this should still shock us. The promise of the land of opportunity is that through *hard work* you can improve your station in life.

So, let me restate what I said in a new way. Since the 1980s, in the United States, you are better off having wealth and *not working* than you are not having wealth and *working hard*.

Buying stocks or buying into real estate investment trusts that add no tangible value to our country brings more prosperity than being a bootstrapping entrepreneur or building those very same homes that the trusts own. That's not my America.

As we continue to reach greater historical dissonance between productivity and wages, which has been spiraling out of control

---

22 Christopher Ingraham, "Massive New Data Set Suggests Economic Inequality is About to Get Even Worse," *The Washington Post,* last modified January 10, 2018, https://www.washingtonpost.com/news/wonk/wp/2018/01/04/massive-new-data-set-suggests-inequality-is-about-to-get-even-worse/?utm_term=.a3713a891bbd.

23 Charles Mudede, "Why It's Misleading to Say the 62 Richest People Have the Same Wealth as Half the World," *The Stranger,* last modified January 18, 2016, https://www.thestranger.com/blogs/slog/2016/01/18/23441405/why-its-misleading-to-say-the-62-richest-people-have-the-same-wealth-as-half-the-world.

24 John W. Schoen, "Study: 1.2 Million Households Lost to Recession," *NBC News,* last modified April 8, 2010, http://www.nbcnews.com/id/36231884/ns/business-eye_on_the_economy/t/study-million-households-lost-recession/.

since the '80s, this equation will continue to get worse and worse. Those who need not work will only continue to make more of the money faster and faster.[25] While most of those who work harder than ever join the precariat.

For those of you in the Baby Boom Generation, you can remember a time when the promise of the land of opportunity was so much clearer. It must be heartbreaking to watch your children and grandchildren struggle in new ways. To take what seems to be a giant leap backward. Even with the much greater expenses we've explored, according to a 2016 report by the New York City comptroller's office, after adjusting for inflation, Millennials today earn about 20 percent less than the generation before them.[26] That is in spite of being the most educated, and indebted, generation our country has ever seen.

For those in the later generations, we have to remember that this is not normal. This is something that must be changed.

If you have $1,000 in savings, you're better off than 57 percent of this country right now.[27] Go back to that quote at the beginning of the book for a moment. If you're one of those people, even with just $1,000 in savings, then you need to speak up before you're one of the people without.

We have to fight for those who don't know how they'll get dinner tonight. They are too busy fighting to survive to hold off foreclosure or keep their families warm; they're very possibly working 70-hour work weeks, and any loss of focus on survival will, for them, mean they're on the street. If you have the means to be active and demanding change you must. There are too few

---

25 "The Productivity–Pay Gap."

26 "Comptroller Stringer Report Finds Millennials Have Faced Toughest Economy since Great Depression," Office of the New York City Comptroller Scott M. Stringer Bureau of Budget, last modified April 26, 2016, https://comptroller.nyc.gov/newsroom/comptroller-stringer-report-finds-millennials-have-faced-toughest-economy-since-great-depression/.

27 Kathleen Elkins, "Here's How Much Money Americans Have in Their Savings Accounts," *CNBC,* last modified September 13, 2017, https://www.cnbc.com/2017/09/13/how-much-americans-at-have-in-their-savings-accounts.html.

of us left and any one of us could be next. We have to recognize that we're one nation, indivisible, even though this country may be falling apart around us at the moment.

There is a silver lining, however.

This is our America and we are a country of reinvention. Economic inequity may well become the Civil Rights Movement of our generation and if we choose to keep this dream alive, and pay the cost it will take to get our democracy back, then we will.

Chapter 2

Full Employment (of the Working Poor)

Let's summarize the crisis so that we're all on the same page.

Wages have been stagnant for all but the upper 10 percent for the past fifty years, productivity and wages no longer travel in tandem, and prevailing attitudes work to racialize, criminalize, and demonize poverty.

Depending on how we measure it, a significant shift took place in the economy over a generation ago. Wages for 90 percent of all workers and employees became decoupled from the ingenuity and productivity of the national economy as a whole. Since the 1970s, wages began to stagnate while worker productivity kept rising—meaning that the lion's share of economic growth went to stockholders, corporations, and financial assets rather than to the people building those products. In fact, the closer you were to physically creating a product or good, the worse off you became during this period. The nation's wealth grew and those who built that wealth had to live on less.

Eventually this shift away from living wages for the working class, combined with the Great Recession, caused our newest American generation to enter the workforce prioritizing *economic stability* over *prosperity*.[28] In other words, the spirit of our next generation is so focused on day-to-day survival, fully focused on fear, that they have lost much of the American spirit, optimism, and hope we've relied on to drive our country forward.

When it wasn't possible to make it on less, we started to compensate for declining spending power with new ways for individuals to take on an ever-greater amount of debt and spend more on social systems that trapped the poor in cycles of poverty. We found a way to create an economic system where we could have full employment *and* a class of working poor with ever greater numbers living below the poverty line.

While it is to be celebrated that in the last few years we have seen some reduction in poverty levels, poverty levels are well above where they were at the start of this century.[29] [30] Yes, about ten million more of us are in poverty than twenty years ago. In addition, the percentage of our population in poverty also remains higher.

In short, the Great Recession saw more people in poverty than any time in at least the last fifty years, and one of the highest poverty rates by percentage we've seen during that period, as well. Yet, we hear today that the economy is doing great, stocks are up, poverty is down, and we're at full employment. Yet, the harsh reality is we're economically worse off than we were before this century started.

Mission not accomplished.

---

28   Hannah Finnie and Simran Jagtiani, "Millennials Crave Economic Stability and Opportunity," Generation Progress, last modified September 2018, http://genprogress.org/wp-content/uploads/2016/09/13114633/Millennials-Crave-Economic-Stability-And-Opportunity-Sept-2016.pdf.

29   Alana Semuels, "New Census Data Shows More Americans Emerging from Poverty," *The Atlantic,* last modified September 12, 2017, https://www.theatlantic.com/business/archive/2017/09/new-census-data-shows-more-americans-emerging-from-poverty/539589/.

30   Ajay Chaudry et al., "Poverty in the United States: 50-Year Trends and Safety Net Impacts," U.S. Department of Health and Human Services, last modified March 2016, https://aspe.hhs.gov/system/files/pdf/154286/50YearTrends.pdf.

Twilight of the Idols

Worst of all, we have lulled our population into inaction by encouraging higher debt levels to temporarily offset the losses in the middle and lower classes. In the past, workers went on strikes because they faced starvation and homelessness. The debt economy is even more insidious. Instead, we created a generation that rather than starving would simply accrue enough debt to make money for the banks and the wealthy for decades. We put people into a twenty-first-century form of indebted servitude, this time on the basis of class.

In the process, we created a bunch of additional financial assets for the wealthy class to make even more money off this debt system—from subprime mortgages to subprime car loans. Of course, as the middle class continues to become worse off, those debts become unpayable. The only world this makes sense in is one where whenever these markets inevitably crash and cause massive suffering to the poor, the federal reserve can step in, print trillions, and protect these financial assets from the losses they should produce.

To put it more simply, we pushed more than 70 percent of Americans into debt they can't pay in a system where the cost of basic goods like housing, education, food, and clothes have doubled, tripled, and quadrupled while wages stagnate or decrease. We then turned these into financial assets, because there weren't enough *good borrowers* left to sustain the profit margins of the rich. When this inevitably failed, the rich got bailed out by the Federal Reserve. And, we moved on as if nothing happened, starting the process again.

As the fable goes, if you want to cook a frog, don't throw it into a boiling pot. It will take action and jump out. Instead, turn up the heat slowly and it will stay in place until it dies. We are that frog, and the structural, systemic debt is the heat.

We've been using the example of higher education, so let's explore the piece it plays in creating today's economic paradigm. A college degree and the mastery it implies used to be seen as a public good: we need a certain amount of educated people across many fields for our society to operate smoothly. The idea was simple—it's in everyone's self-interest that our institutions train doctors, lawyers, accountants, and engineers, so *even if I'm not one, I don't mind that we all pay a little for their education.* You might not have needed a college degree, and might not have wanted one, but you understood why some did, and why it needed to be affordable. Now, college is something that banks and government agencies will lend you lots of money for, and there's very little emphasis (if any at all) on it being a public service, as opposed to a private luxury or need.

Maybe you recall Mitt Romney's advice to young people in the 2012 Presidential campaign: "I would encourage you to get as much education as your parents can afford."[31] Even that advice points to the fact that college is incredibly expensive, and not necessarily possible for anyone who wants it. Worst, it essentially says class should determine your education level. For the record, I think Romney is aptly pointing out the truth here: we've created two castes here. While we aren't removing education as an option entirely, we are saying that if you're not from a wealthy family and you want to be educated you're going to probably live in a cycle of debt the rest of your life.

There's less emphasis on your degree as a public good, and more emphasis on all of the loans that you can acquire to get it. And chances are that how you go to college, or even whether or not you get to go to college, has less to do with your hopes for a particular career than it does to do with money. And debt.

In every aspect of American life (housing, automobiles, health, and so on), we've been conditioned to take on larger and larger amounts of debt in order to have the things we've been told are essential for "the good life" and that are, in fact, essential to modern life. Since 86 percent of Americans rely on cars to get to work, we've created another subprime debt bubble, just like

---

31   Pat Garofalo, "Romney: Students Should Get 'As Much Education as They Can Afford,'" Think Progress, last modified June 29, 2012, https://thinkprogress.org/romney-students-should-get-as-much-education-as-they-can-afford-2b9f1275b85b/.

housing, to accommodate this critical need without fixing the underlying problem.[32] Now, just as before, we're seeing massive reliance on subprime loans being almost a quarter of all loans. Yet, the same financial predators that leveraged the American subprime mortgages are flocking into this *booming* market even as default rates soar.[33] Even while Steve Eismen, the man now famous for predicting the housing collapse, is telling every news agency he can that this is happening again.

In countries with single-payer health care, the health of every citizen is considered a social asset, so everyone has access to health care. The idea is that *it's in my self-interest that my neighbor is healthy, so I don't mind that we're all paying a little for health care.* In the U.S., medical bills are the chief reason for people declaring bankruptcy, and the people who aren't declaring bankruptcy are making monthly payments to hospitals in order to pay down debt they've accumulated—and while those payment plans make the debt more affordable on a monthly basis, all of those payments and expenses also get added into the ever-growing list of bills that keep us on the precipice, one debt payment away from disaster.[34]

Of course, the best icon of the new debt is the ubiquitous credit card. How many people do you know who have maxed out one or more cards just buying the basics for a decent life—gas in the tank, shoes for the kids, groceries in the pantry, etc.? It seems that every business you need to utilize has a credit card that can help you get what you need, and pay it off later; whether you're at the gas station, the dentist office, a veterinary clinic, or

32 Brian McKenzie, "Who Drives to Work? Commuting by Automobile in the United States: 2013," United States Census Bureau, last modified August 2015, https://www.census.gov/content/dam/Census/library/publications/2015/acs/acs-32.pdf.

33 Cecile Gutscher, "Subprime Auto Debt is Booming Even as Defaults Soar," Bloomberg, last modified February 1, 2018, https://www.bloomberg.com/news/articles/2018-02-02/never-mind-defaults-debt-backed-by-subprime-auto-loans-is-hot.

34 Maurie Backman, "This is the No. 1 Reason Americans File for Bankruptcy," The Motley Fool, last modified May 1, 2017, https://www.fool.com/retirement/2017/05/01/this-is-the-no-1-reason-americans-file-for-bankrup.aspx.

a mechanic, there's a credit card to help you in the moment. And because you don't have any money saved, there's a good chance that credit card *is* the only way to get what you need immediately. You'll just have to think about the debt, and the ever-growing interest, when you can.

As of the end of 2017, the average American household had $173,995 in mortgage debt, $46,597 in student debt, $27,669 in auto loan debt, and $15,654 in credit card debt.[35] A combined total of $263,915 in debt with a median American household income of $56,516.[36]

The consequence of these economic changes is that America has become a nation of debt rather than opportunity. Again, 73 percent of us will live, work, and die in debt. We're caught in an endless cycle, working long hours and neglecting all of the other parts of our lives in hopes that we can keep debt at bay.

Innovation and ingenuity—which have uniquely defined our national character, and for which the rest of the world envies us—are on the decline in the generation currently coming of age and entering into adulthood. Some would say we just don't have time for those anymore. I say, these national traits are going away not because our culture has changed or because young Americans don't want to move forward with this spirit, this drive for opportunity, and a better future. It's because they're living in massive education debt which is augmented by the other kinds of debt mentioned above—housing, transportation, health care, and consumer debt—and they have to work to make their monthly payments on these debts, which can rival the cost of housing. Again, we're faced with the specter of making the equivalent of a monthly mortgage payment twice over: once for rent and

---

35 Maurie Backman, "Here's a Breakdown of the Average American's Household Debt," The Motley Fool, last modified December 24, 2017, https://www.fool.com/retirement/2017/12/24/heres-a-breakdown-of-the-average-americans-househo.aspx.

36 Emmie Martin, "Here's How Much the Average American Earns at Every Age," *CNBC*, last modified August 24, 2017, https://www.cnbc.com/2017/08/24/how-much-americans-earn-at-every-age.html.

again for educational debt—and yet, having no real estate assets appreciating in value over the years to show for it.

Thoughts of opportunity and growth have been replaced with strategies for paying off debt.

We've been told the Great Recession is over. If you're exceptionally wealthy, then yes, the recession has been over for quite some time. Yet, more Americans are in poverty today than was the case before the Great Recession; the debt continues to build and the once indomitable American optimism is being replaced with cynicism and turmoil. We've gotten to a point where even those who are super-wealthy—people like Nick Hanauer, Warren Buffett, Chuck Collins, Bill Gates, Sr., and the group known as the Patriotic Millionaires—are advocating against their short-term economic interest, because they too understand we are headed toward collapse. The Patriotic Millionaires arose in 2010, after the 2008 collapse, as a network of high-net worth Americans who are aware that the concentration of wealth and power has one inevitable conclusion if we don't fix it: destabilization.[37]

That's the outcome, but here and now it comes down to one simple point. The income has flatlined, the costs have gone up, and virtually all Americans must take on a necessary amount of debt to pay for basic needs in a modern society. We created something new. A class of people who work full-time and live in poverty. A group known as the working poor.

*

"Nobody should be working full time and not making it. Nobody in our society...the richest country, the richest nation in the history of the world, should feel as frightened and anxious and insecure as so many people do today."

—Robert Reich, Former Secretary of Labor, *Saving Capitalism*

---

37   "About Us: The Patriotic Millionaires," Patriotic Millionaires, accessed November 27, 2018, https://patrioticmillionaires.org/about/.

Brayden W.B. Olson

The state of America today is a society that's no longer the land of opportunity and upward mobility, as the 44th President observed. It's a country of systemic debt as a nation and as a people.

We've become a dystopian nation where so many of us live with the fear that any one disruption—a layoff or a medical illness—could leave us and our entire family broken. We live in a nation that rewards wealth over hard work. A nation moving closer and closer to having two classes—the have-nots and the have-yachts—with a diminishing middle class.

Without reform, our country will continue down a road that looks more like a caste system with each passing year. The rich get richer, the poor get poorer, and with our elections up for sale, power continues to concentrate toward the few. For sale, because more than 90 percent of elections are decided simply by who raised the most money.

I agree with conservatives who take pride in a capitalist market where hard work, risk, innovation, and productivity lead to great financial wealth. As discussed above, today's system no longer even remotely resembles that. It's been replaced instead by a system where we've turned debt into a financial asset. We've forced a majority of Americans into debt to grow this "asset" made up of sub-prime mortgage, auto, and other loans. We turned education into a federally backed debt asset for private companies. And, when these systems inevitably default, we pay out the banks from the Federal Reserve.

We've replaced innovation with debt and capitalism with a federal government that makes sure wealth can speculate and grow without ever taking risk. Paid for by taxes on the working poor.

Pointing to a few red herring examples who have escaped this system changes nothing about the reality of the system we have created. Yes, a few people have gone from being members of the very poor to being members of the very rich, but if anything, it's those exceptions to the rule that prove the point. It's like saying that because we have a lottery that moves 1 in 10,000 people from the lower class to the upper class, we don't have a class system at all. The facts are shocking. In one generation, economic mobility has dropped to less than half of what it was before. 92 percent of Boomers earned more than their parents, but less than half (45 percent) of their children, Millennials, will. Consider that for a second. That means as a whole, as Americans, most of our next generation will actually move *down* the socioeconomic ladder.[38]

*

If we want to restore economic vitality to the United States (and economic vitality necessarily includes social mobility), our government must pursue two principles: first, that all citizens—individuals, families, communities, and institutions—have the ability to pass on savings, not debt, to the next generations; and, second, that meaningful work (which is safe, well-paid, and socially constructive) be available to all those who are willing to take it on and work hard to succeed. This means meaningful reform to increase average American incomes, decrease expenses that are absolutely necessary to modern life, or a combination of both.

This doesn't require handouts. It requires re-stacking the deck to allow for a capitalist, free market economy that can work without structured indebtedness and simply ensuring a market stays open and competitive without corporate, political, and economic consolidation. The quickest way to get there is to re-hitch the wagon of wages and income to the draft horse of a productive, twenty-first-century economy.

If it had not been for these debt markets, our democracy would have likely already fixed our capitalist markets. When people can't eat, or educate their children, they strike.

Now that all of this is starting to come out into the open, and Americans are awakening to the truth, it's become clear that we

---

38   Lawrence F. Katz and Alan B. Krueger, "Documenting Decline in U.S. Economic Mobility," *Science,* last modified April 24, 2017, http://science.sciencemag.org/content/early/2017/04/21/science.aan3264.full.

need more than small changes. We need systematic alterations. Worse, we have another massive challenge on the horizon: we only have about a decade left before automation replaces half the jobs that currently exist in this country.[39]

Since this is our first time discussing automation, I am going to share the definition I use here. For many, the threat automation poses is either very well-known or has already impacted their lives. When I use the term automation in this book, I am most often referring to automation and artificial intelligence. What's the difference? Automation involves the superhuman machines replacing blue collar, working-class jobs bit by bit each years, such as factory work and construction work. We can do more with fewer humans with each additional innovation. Artificial intelligence is the computational intelligence behind software and other computer systems that are replacing white collar jobs. In many areas, they already surpass our capabilities, but most experts agree we aren't far away from the point where computer intelligence will surpass human intelligence. In the near future, you'll see stable, highly educated workers like lawyers disappear too.[40] We are already seeing reductions in these industries as AI software advances. The threat we face is a universal American middle-class problem and should be treated as such. Researchers at Oxford University, analyzing how susceptible jobs are to computerization, found that 47 percent of the jobs in the U.S. are likely to disappear to automation in the next ten to twenty years. That was five years ago.[41]

For now, let's just say these forces work together, because automation and AI lead to an ever smaller percentage of citizens

39   Carl Benedikt Frey and Michael A. Osborne, "The Future of Employment: How Susceptible Are Jobs to Computerisation?" The Oxford Martin School at the University of Oxford, last modified September 17, 2013, https://www.oxfordmartin.ox.ac.uk/downloads/academic/The_Future_of_Employment.pdf.

40   Erin Winick, "Lawyer-Bots Are Shaking Up Jobs," *MIT Technology Review,* last modified December 12, 2017, https://www.technologyreview.com/s/609556/lawyer-bots-are-shaking-up-jobs/.

41   Frey and Osborne, "The Future of Employment: How Susceptible Are Jobs to Computerisation?"

who fall into the category of people who have more than a thousand dollars or so in savings, and who can afford to take an hour or two of their week, let alone a whole day off, to be politically active. And that is the crux of it.

AI and automation play but one critical piece in a larger puzzle. I will explore that puzzle in various ways from a variety of perspectives and research throughout this book, but I will do my best to summarize it now.

Since the 1970s and 1980s, economic inequality (consolidation), automation, taxes, globalization, and our bipartisan, winner-takes-all political system have all come together to create one inevitable outcome: to create an America that for the first time in her history will see a generation become worse off than the last. A generation of children who will have a poorer economic standing than their parents for the first time since we founded this country.

As automation has grown, the productivity a corporation can generate off a single worker has grown dramatically.[42] Every year, companies see more productivity/gain per worker, workers see declined or negligible wage increases, and power shifts ever more from labor to owner. In steady progression, fewer people *make things* and instead more room is created for financiers to ever grow these businesses. Now, the financial sector is the largest part of the U.S. economy, which both Democrats and Republicans have served since the 1980s.[43]

That means more of our economy every year is based on financial instruments than the actual building of things that these financial instruments are supposed to support. Once both sides of Congress got on board, we've seen a continued slide toward a tax code that supports having wealth, as opposed to work. As already

---

42 "The Productivity–Pay Gap."

43 Christopher Witko, "How Wall Street Became a Big Chunk of the U.S. Economy —and When the Democrats Signed On," *The Washington Post,* last modified March 29, 2016, https://www.washingtonpost.com/news/monkey-cage/wp/2016/03/29/how-wall-street-became-a-big-chunk-of-the-u-s-economy-and-when-the-democrats-signed-on/?utm_term=.440e0068d946.

mentioned, data included in *Capital in the Twenty-First Century* reveal that, all told, you're likely to become wealthier from having wealth and not working than from participating in the working economy.[44]

To support that system, we built and support a tax code that taxes income gained from working (income tax) at a higher rate than income gained on wealth building more wealth (capital gains).

Globalization is, on the whole, positive and most certainly unavoidable. Yet, in our current political and economic paradigm it too becomes a critical part of the picture. You could outsource your work anywhere in the world, further decreasing the influence of labor. For those individuals and businesses with enough wealth, this also became a way to more easily hide their wealth and avoid taxation on it. Once more, global powers that had established oligopolies or monopolies in one region can now spread that influence globally with much greater ease.

Since the 1980s, those with over $100M in wealth have tripled their ownership of the U.S. total economy. The other 99 percent of households have seen a decline in wealth.[45] For all the reasons above, wealth continues a steady progression of consolidation globally—away from those who work toward those who already have.

What turns this from an economic problem into a political one is that statesmen and women of the past put their efforts toward keeping our beacon of hope alive in times of war and ensuring our country remained stable and united in times of strife and instability. We aimed to keep our country economically strong, but in a system where 91 percent of elections are won by

---

44 Ingraham, "Massive New Data Set Suggests Economic Inequality Is About to Get Even Worse."

45 Steve Hargreaves, "Rich, Really Rich, and Ultra Rich," *CNN Business,* last modified June 3, 2014, https://money.cnn.com/2014/06/01/luxury/rich-wealth-gap/index.html.

whoever raises the most money, our democracy has a price tag.[46] This is where the consolidation matters. 67 percent of election funding comes from major donors and PACs now, with just 27 percent coming from small donors. That means the major donors decide who has the most money and that person takes the seat 91 percent of the time.

As I will explore in this book, there is only one issue that underpins all the others. Everything we care about or fight about stems in some way from this cycle of economic inequality. That's why our politicians fight over these social issues. They want to win elections, not solve the issues.

And that is how these trends create a horrifying snowball with an irrevocable outcome. The snowball is that economic consolidation means fewer people have a voice in who runs our country. The politicians choose to either lose their job or work for those interests. If they choose to lose their job, someone else will gladly replace them. In turn, those politicians legislate in ways that further the economic advantage of those already wealthy who then, in turn, ensure they have the proper funding to win their next election.

The irrevocable outcome if we can't change this snowball? We become the first generation in American history to be worse off than the last, and in the age of automation, we have to watch the country we love economically collapse in on itself.

And we do so while other countries readily prepare themselves to take our place. China, which already boasts double the rate of Millennial homeownership and a middle class that is strengthening every year, would be glad to become the new seat of entrepreneurship and economic power in the world. And even though our government would have us believe that we will never give up that station, we're well on the way to doing just that.

There was once another economy and nation that led the world in innovation, trade, entrepreneurship, economic output,

---

46 Wesley Lowery, "91% of the Time the Better-Financed Candidate Wins. Don't Act Surprised," *The Washington Post*, last modified April 4, 2014, https://www.washingtonpost.com/news/the-fix/wp/2014/04/04/think-money-doesnt-matter-in-elections-this-chart-says-youre-wrong/.

and productivity, and it did so for well over one hundred years. It was the undisputed heavyweight in the world. At its peak, it saw a massive rise in living standards—just like we did here, in the United States. Then, over the course of about thirty years, things began to change dramatically. Leisure, not entrepreneurship, became a pastime of the elites. The working class began to protest as their struggles became more and more difficult, their protests coming from unrest over their economic issues. How short our memories. Our grandparents watched the 20th century decline as Great Britain saw its empire disappear as the once-great nation lost its status as one of the world's economic, political, and military superpowers.[47]

Yet, we have already forgotten these lessons, and we appear ready to repeat the same course within the span of hardly a lifetime.

Solutions abound. We have every ability to make different choices and choose a path that will revitalize our entrepreneurship, make education, housing and medicine affordable again, and lead the world once. But we cannot do it without addressing a system that rewards wealth, not work. And we can't address that without the campaign reform that will be discussed in the final chapters of this book.

As individuals, we must stop feeling shame over our circumstances, for it's what keeps so many of us silent. The dominant narrative is that only a few of us are struggling, and they must therefore be solely to blame for their misfortune. It's this narrative that allows us to doubt the quicksand around our feet. The ground has changed in fundamental ways not felt by prior generations, but that is exactly why our youth today are the first that will, as a generation, have lower economic opportunity than their parents.

---

47 "Economic History of the United Kingdom: 1900-1945," Wikipedia, accessed November 29, 2018, https://en.wikipedia.org/wiki/Economic_history_of_the_United_Kingdom#1900-1945.

Twilight of the Idols

We need candidates across the board whose uncompromising value is to restore the United States as a center of economic opportunity for those committed to hard work and innovation.

In 2012, just a few years after the worst economic downturn in more than half a century, *Forbes* declared the American dream "still very much alive." The evidence? The magazine said that 70 percent of the Forbes 400 richest Americans—all billionaires—were "self-made" by its definition.[48] But an analysis by United for a Fair Economy pointed out that only 35 percent of the billionaires on the list were born into a lower middle-class or middle-class background, fewer than half of what was being claimed. Rather, almost 70 percent came from prosperous families, and fully 21 percent were born with enough wealth to qualify for the list by birth.[49]

That year, the wealthiest 159 people owned the same wealth as the poorer half of the world's population. In 2013, that number became 92. In 2014, 80. In 2015, 62.[50] By 2017, that number became just 8 men.[51] Like clockwork, we are watching the slow and steady progression to an unprecedented concentration of wealth that will first destabilize the American way of life and, ultimately, the global economy.

Capitalism is a phenomenal model, but one that also has a breaking point. Take Walmart, for example. As the Walton family's fortune continues to amass, they hold food donations at Thanksgiving and other holidays for their own employees because

48 Luisa Kroll, "The Forbes 400: The Richest People in America," *Forbes,* last modified September 19, 2012, https://www.forbes.com/sites/luisakroll/2012/09/19/the-forbes-400-the-richest-people-in-america/#c749f9f4fd26.

49 Robert Frank, "Did the Forbes 400 Billionaires Really 'Build That'?" *CNBC,* last modified September 25, 2012, https://www.cnbc.com/id/49167533.

50 Larry Elliott, "Richest 62 People as Wealthy as Half of World's Population, Says Oxfam," *The Guardian,* last modified January 18, 2016, https://www.theguardian.com/business/2016/jan/18/richest-62-billionaires-wealthy-half-world-population-combined.

51 "Just 8 Men Own Same Wealth as Half the World," Oxfam International, last modified January 16, 2017, https://www.oxfam.org/en/pressroom/pressreleases/2017-01-16/just-8-men-own-same-wealth-half-world.

they struggle to eat on the wages they are paid and food stamps they receive.[52] There is just no way such a model can continue into the future. If full employment at the largest and most profitable companies in our country means poverty, then something is seriously broken.

This isn't an argument against enterprise or capitalism. In fact, we have great examples from our past that build economic prosperity for individual workers and growth for the entire economy as a whole. Henry Ford, for example, strengthened the middle class with his innovations. His employees could afford to be his customers. That is the American Dream.

It wasn't about quarterly profits and distributions. We had vision. Companies were founded to thrive for decades, be passed down, build our community and country in meaningful ways. Today, we found *products* and *apps* not companies, and you're looked at as if you are insane if your plan is anything other than to build a product, get some *traction*, and have it be acquired by a big company in four years or less.

As I've said before, the wagon of productivity and wages must be re-hitched if we want a sustainable, twenty-first-century economy where the caliber of and commitment toward one's work can define who gets ahead in our country. Our efforts, our hard work, need to be capable of ensuring us the opportunity for a future that includes happiness, freedom from debt, and equality. And, right now, that's not the state of affairs for most Americans.

For those who believe in rugged capitalism and free markets, you too should be passionate about this change. In the model we have today, in a desperate attempt to keep the wheels moving, the government must increase taxes to support programs like food stamps for increasing numbers of Americans *who are fully employed*. If you want lower taxes, and less government intervention, then you also need economic inequality, lower

---

52 Jana Kasperkevic, "Walmart Workers Increasingly Rely on Food Banks, Report Says," *The Guardian,* last modified November 21, 2014, https://www.theguardian.com/money/us-money-blog/2014/nov/21/walmart-workers-rely-on-food-banks-report.

debt, and higher economic opportunity as well. The companies can either pay the employees through living wages or pay the government to turn around and then pay the employees their food stamps.

What we need to accept: corruption at the top of a pyramid spreads misery throughout.

So far, we've been discussing the biggest problem in the economy today—productive work that no longer pays a decent wage or salary. At the other end of the wealth pyramid, at the very top, we have an equally disturbing phenomenon: the no-risk investment that automatically pays a handsome return. Simply put, those with enough wealth get access to deals, investments, and opportunities that the rest of the country never do. This is exactly what happened in the financial meltdown that torched the economy in 2008, and yet the wealthiest walked away without impact.

If your bets win, you win. If you're "too big to fail" and you lose, the Federal Reserve pays you out at the expense of the public's future tax dollars.

For the public, your home became a poker chip that speculators could bet on and win every time. If you got out alive, you kept your house, but went into deeper debt and *won* a future of higher taxes. If you lost, you lost your home and still inherited a future of higher taxes.

Up is down, and black is white. People work forty hours a week, and yet they need public assistance to make ends meet. Or, forty hours isn't enough, so a sixty or seventy-hour work week becomes their norm. On the flip side are business deals that are so big that, when they fail, the public treasury has to clean up the mess, or else the entire economy goes down the drain. Obscene wealth can safely invest in real estate in ways that the rest of the population can't. Wall Street firms wrecked the global economy and gave us the Great Recession. Their punishment? Recover at taxpayer expense, and then have access to near 0 percent financing from the federal government for almost a decade.

Brayden W.B. Olson

The Wall Street financial engineering is generally made to be so complicated that most people can't understand they're structured to be safe bets for the billionaire dealmakers, even if the deals blow up down the road. As a result, more and more money is going into securitizing questionable mortgages (and other questionable financial instruments), and, in turn, less money is going into funding the beginning or expansion of legitimate, productive businesses that grow our country, community, and GDP. The big dealmakers don't suffer from this, so let's go back to focusing on them for a moment since they're acquiring most of the money anyway.

The most famous example of this financial engineering was what happened in the 2008 collapse. When dealmakers couldn't put any more virtually guaranteed, safe money-making deals on the table, they had to expand their pool to subprime mortgages. For those who haven't seen the movie *The Big Short*, subprime mortgages simply mean mortgages that shouldn't be funded in the first place (alternatively explained as s*** loans in the film). Subprimes almost always load an individual or a family with what will quickly become an unmanageable amount of debt. They required what may have started as a reasonable monthly payment, but then encountered balloon payments or rising variable rates that the given family simply couldn't be expected to make. Eventually that meant a family would, almost without question, be foreclosed upon. They created ever increasingly complex financial products on these loans to the point where $50M in loans could have $1B betting on it (called Synthetic CDOs). All so that investors and the American people could be swindled for fees.

Those bankers took advantage of our families and communities. The dealmakers took advantage of teachers, firefighters, nurses, engineers, and millions of other good people in this country whose only crime was not having finance degrees and working on Wall Street. In the end, the bankers all got their bonuses secured by the American taxpayer.

When this system failed, many among the poor and middle classes lost their homes. But the makers of the deals, the originators of the loans, had skimmed big bonuses off the top and made their profits on the front end, knowing full well that most of their mortgages would blow up and lead to foreclosure. The Wall Street catchphrase was, and is: IBGYBG—*I'll be gone, you'll be gone* (and we'll let someone else clean up our mess). Even many wealthy Americans, who simply fell short of the "aristocratic" level of wealth, lost massive amounts of value in the properties they owned. On the other hand, the aristocracy, those whose funds Wall Street bankers use to speculate, were handed a check to cover their investments—funded by the lower classes' tax dollars.

Eight million people lost their jobs. Six million lost their homes. The cycle has even started again under a new name, "bespoke tranche opportunity."[53] That's right, banks picked right back up after the crisis, rebranded the Synthetic CDO, and are making profits again on what Bloomberg News identified as the same products that got us into the housing crisis.[54] Why? Because they made a killing off it the first time and only working people suffered the consequence. Reward received by one group, risk shouldered by another.

There's a lot of money to be made in keeping our economy in turmoil: preventing a free market, keeping monopolies secure, and continuing a political system that is unintentionally tied to the interests of these companies.

Chuck Collins, an heir to the Oscar Meyer fortune, unburdened himself of the trust fund he'd inherited early in life, giving away $500,000. Since then, he's been a tireless advocate for a just economy, which he defines as a system that works for all. That

---

53   Lisa Abramowicz, "A Synthetic CDO by Any Other Name Is Still Risky," Bloomberg, last modified February 3, 2017, https://www.bloomberg.com/gadfly/articles/2017-02-03/a-synthetic-cdo-by-any-other-name-is-still-risky.

54   Sridhar Natarajan, Dakin Campbell, and Alastair Marsh, "Citi Is Bringing Back One of the Most Infamous Bets of the Credit Crisis," Bloomberg, last modified September 26, 2017, https://www.bloomberg.com/news/articles/2017-09-26/as-synthetic-cdos-roar-back-a-young-citi-trader-makes-her-name.

is, when the economy is doing well, the whole of society shares in the good times. Instead, Collins has observed that since 1982 the wealthiest three families have seen their wealth increase by 6,000 percent while the median household wealth has decreased by 3 percent over the same period.[55]

As Supreme Court Justice Louis Brandeis said, "We can have democracy in this country, or we can have great wealth concentrated in the hands of a few, but we can't have both." In my view, it's clear that sooner or later, a person who is many orders of magnitude more powerful than everyone else will start to use their power to get whatever they want. Even good men and women will do so without really intending it. In a very real way, that's what's been playing out in our political system. Today, we have a nanny state for the wealthiest 1 percent of our society, and a rugged individualism for everyone else.

Wealth should not guarantee more wealth. Investments should carry with them risk and, when successful, they should add to the productive capacity of the economy, not render it asunder. Speculative capital, or at least a large portion thereof, needs to be legislatively pushed back toward start-ups and sectors that grow our productive economy. There are numerous approaches we could take. From offering tax breaks like the U.K.'s SEIS programme for these early stage investments, to reducing the number of Wall Street instruments, to taking a hard look at how we could make real estate investment more crowdfunded. It won't require one simple piece of legislation, but an ongoing intentional effort to once again push our country's investment toward true growth and value investing.

Most of this chapter has dealt with the financial health of an economy that's been slowly but surely concentrating wealth at an accelerating pace since the '80s. Yet, beneath the myths, the idols, and the media we find a world of living human beings who are

---

55   Chuck Collins, "The Wealth of America's Three Richest Families Grew by 6,000% since 1982," *The Guardian,* last modified October 31, 2018, https://www.theguardian.com/commentisfree/2018/oct/31/us-wealthiest-families-dynasties-governed-by-rich.

near their breaking point. A group of humans who would have already broken if not allowed to go so deeply into debt peonage, but for whom the interests on those debts could soon take them over the precipice.

I know this picture seems bleak, but we live in the wealthiest country in the history of the world. Our output and wealth have continued to grow. In fact, we probably have more now than we have ever had.

Let's say that again. We are watching our children become the first generation in American history to be financially worse off than their parents during a time when we have more than ever. The problem isn't our progress or technology or prosperity. It's the new rules governing the game: the anti-free market systems that are taking away the American promise that through hard work our country is the land of opportunity.

That means we can do something about it. Are you ready for the how? Fiscal conservatives and small government supporters, stay with me for just a minute and I will share why this is the solution for you as well.

Universal Basic Income. UBI can mean a lot of different things; there is *no one size fits all* that would work for every country. However, mostly commonly, UBI is the idea of providing income to all citizens to ensure basic needs like food, shelter, and medicine are met.

For someone who wants small government, this might sound like a nightmare. However, it could replace Welfare, Social Security, Disability Insurance, Medicare, Section 8 Housing, and dozens of other programs. Under a simplified system, these agencies and bureaucracies would disappear, which would in and of itself could save money.

For those who share my enthusiasm with reducing our deficit and stimulating growth, this is the plan for you. In fact, recent research on the economic impact of UBI indicated that a UBI of just $1,000 per month would increase GDP by 12 percent over the next seven years.[56] With the right policies and planning, this economic growth can be used to get Americans and America out of debt. In fact, the research also indicates that every $1 that goes to wage earners would increase our economy by $1.21, while every $1 going to high-income earners would add only $.39 to the overall economy. The more we invest in hard working Americans, the more our economy will work.

But, wouldn't people stop working? Actually, pilot programs have shown that less than 1 percent of people stopped working, and most of those did so to take care of children.[57] In fact, our current programs have shown to encourage much less participation. Why? Because in many cases these programs actually pay people to stay home, because taking jobs that pay only slightly more than your welfare (after taxes and transportation) can mean making even less money. By taking jobs in our current system, some people lose money and we, as an economy, lose. Under UBI, you always have *more* incentive to work.

UBI is a capitalistic solution. It will provide more incentive to work than current programs, stimulate economic growth, reduce bureaucracy, and give us a chance to reduce our deficit through intelligent planning. There will still be the rich, middle class, and poor, but our economy will be more stable because the gap will no longer be between rich and poverty.

This single adjustment could help begin to get America back on the track we once experienced in the '50s, '60s, and '70s. UBI isn't the entire solution. Policy is complicated and the real solutions will be in getting more statesmen and women into office, which I will address in my final chapters. However, UBI could be the step we need today to save our middle class and the American Dream.

56   Thomas Straubhaar, "On the Economics of a Universal Basic Income," *Intereconomics* 52, no. 2 (2017): 74-80, accessed November 29, 2018, https://archive.intereconomics.eu/year/2017/2/on-the-economics-of-a-universal-basic-income/.

57   Abhijit V. Banerjee et al., "Debunking the Stereotype of the Lazy Welfare Recipient: Evidence from Cash Transfer Programs," *The World Bank Research Observer* 32, no. 2 (2017): 155-184, last modified August 30, 2017, https://academic.oup.com/wbro/article/32/2/155/4098285.

Twilight of the Idols

Today we live in one of the most economically difficult times since the Great Depression, with the biggest divide between the have and have nots. In such a time, just remember that when you are a hardworking person and you still struggle, that should not bring you shame. Most of America is struggling right along with you. Remember, you are not alone.

Chapter 3

Where the World Comes to Learn

It's a story we have all heard. The wealthy from around the world send their children here to study. It must follow then that our education system is the best in the world.

The truth, unfortunately, isn't the case. Rather, we learn that our K-12 public education is in chaos, and while our higher education system still has a strong reputation it's still a three-tiered system. A few elite colleges, a weakening public university system, and an overlooked community college system.

Let's begin to unravel this next idol. My guess is that you've heard that this, that, or some other country's students are significantly outperforming us in math, reading, writing, and/or science. Generally, the name you'll hear is China, Singapore, or South Korea. Perhaps the Scandinavian countries. Even if you haven't been to school in some time, rumors of our students underperforming in comparison to other countries has probably reached your ears. Why is this?

To be clear, both of my parents are public school teachers, as are many others in my family, so this isn't a knock at teachers. There are hundreds of thousands of talented teachers struggling to make sure our kids get the best education they can, at all levels of the system, from kindergarten on through graduate school.

Twilight of the Idols

The amazing public servants we call teachers are as trapped by the status quo as our students. Everything that follows in this chapter is a discussion on the system, not our teachers.

Let's start by taking a look at our perspectives. Most of you reading this came out of the American school system, or maybe you're even working for it now, and you've been led to believe that your education offered you the knowledge you needed to find that much-promised opportunity, the American Dream. By virtue of your hard work, you could get what you needed to from the school system—this is probably how your parents felt if they raised you in America, and it's probably how you feel about your own children or grandchildren. Why? Because we're trained to believe in it. For the sake of our own confidence in ourselves, our futures, and our country, it seems like we almost have to believe in it.

Now you fall into one of two categories. You're either an American who isn't in school—in which case you're paying more per student in taxes than all but four of the thirty-four most modernized countries in the world[58] (those are Austria, Luxenberg, Norway, and Switzerland by the way). Or, you're a student in school today who has no control over the quality of your education, and maybe you know deep down that it isn't preparing you for the real world. And you know what, parents? I think you know deep down too that our school system isn't preparing your kids for the real world, too. You just don't want to believe it, and I don't blame you.

So, let's start with you—the graduated worker. Your kids, grandkids, and/or nieces and nephews rely on this education system for their future. Whether they've relied on public school or private school to lead them into the future, they've worked hard and made their way forward. Maybe they're already in college, and some savings accounts have been cleared out to help them

---

58 "Education at a Glance 2014: OECD Indicators," OECD Publishing, accessed November 29, 2018, https://read.oecd-ilibrary.org/education/education-at-a-glance-2014_eag-2014-en#page4.

manage the finances—assuming you didn't clear out those savings accounts for private schools to begin with, if you were already doubting public schools. Chances are, their higher education is happening on American soil, and that means there's a hefty bill attached, but nobody doubts that that final degree will be worth the investment because the difference in income between those with and without a degree has reached an all-time high.[59] All that money, or debt, will be worth it in the end—they'll have great jobs that they can invest in and care about, and they'll make enough money to pay off the debt before they know it. That's how it's supposed to work, and you're sure that's how it will work for your incredibly smart and talented children. College was the next step, after all, and now they're on their way to success.

While we've paid the equivalent of a Lamborghini for their education, a Toyota Camry has just shown up in the driveway. (No offense to the Camry, of course.) As mentioned, we're paying more than all but four small countries per student, but our students are ranking average or below average across virtually every international comparison.[60] It's too late to return the car, but sooner or later, you're going to be upset about it. So, what can you do? Well, we'll get to that in a minute.

Let's get back to our second set of readers before we get too far ahead of ourselves.

If you're a student in high school, you're learning facts, figures, dates, and names that could as easily be Googled. In an information age, when we need to be focused on teaching critical thinking to our children, we're throttled by curriculums, government standards, and radically slow adoption of technology.

Again, our teachers are great teachers, but we fail to support them with appropriate resources and subject matter experts who could help in key disciplines. We also throttle their curriculum

---

59   Rugaber, "Pay Gap between College Grads and Everyone Else at a Record."

60   Drew DeSilver, "U.S. Students' Academic Achievement Still Lags That of Their Peers in Many Other Countries," Pew Research Center, last modified February 15, 2017, http://www.pewresearch.org/fact-tank/2017/02/15/u-s-students-internationally-math-science/.

to be about test preparation as opposed to life preparation. The whole system—from student, to teacher, to administration—is oriented to ace a test. Not because the test is aligned with your future career success, but because the federal government writes a check to fund the schools in your state based on having a state test in place. And it's also possible that those test scores will determine future budgets, the careers of teachers, and resources for your little brothers and sisters. They could, if they're low enough, even be an incentive to close your school.

On average, an American kid today will now take 112 mandatory, standardized tests before graduating high school.[61] That's more than 8.5 tests per year—or, as an average, about one per month you're actually in school from kindergarten to graduation. While the idea behind the 2002 No Child Left Behind law was great, which was to be able to identify and bring up low performing schools to an even standard by having tests in place, the actual application has dramatically accelerated this crippling obsession.

It's why if you're a student today, you're cramming for tests, and your teachers are teaching to tests that may or may not be any use at all to your future. How in the world could administrations or teachers help teach students the skills they really need to succeed when they have to scramble from one test to another? Let alone find time to learn and adapt new, critical technology that could help enhance actual learning?

Thus, our K-12 system is broken: structured entirely around standardized tests rather than student outcomes. That's like having a non-profit that is measured by how much money they spend rather than how many people they help. Or, for that matter, an economy that's health is measured by stock prices when fewer people can even afford to buy stocks than ten years ago, or by the

---

61 Lyndsey Layton, "Study Says Standardized Testing Is Overwhelming Nation's Public Schools," *The Washington Post*, last modified October 24, 2015, https://www.washingtonpost.com/local/education/study-says-standardized-testing-is-overwhelming-nations-public-schools/2015/10/24/8a22092c-79ae-11e5-a958-d889faf561dc_story.html?utm_term=.3e927ec25e80.

employment rate when more and more fully employed people are falling below the poverty line. That would be insane, wouldn't it?

If that's the problem with our K-12 system, then what's wrong with our universities? They must be the best in the world, because people pay big money from around the world to come here, right? Well, the truth is it is hard to say either way.

A university's quality is generally measured on the likelihood of employers to hire applicants from a certain school or department. Logically, that makes sense since the purpose of an education for most students is to find stronger career placement. Many university departments have web pages that advertise the successes of their graduates and the great success that they've gone on to find—it's a way to attract new students, and it's the metric that determines their success. In other words, we're talking about brand reputation. On the other hand, our public education system, K-12, is measured by how our students perform on tests when compared to students of the same age around the world.

One of the ways we measure things is qualitative, based on how we feel about a thing, and the other is quantitative, based on the numerical, statistical facts behind it; another way to think of it is to say that we can measure based on feeling and anecdotal evidence, or based on flat statistics and absolutes. Think of the ways that students put together their college applications: there are pieces of an application that come together and require qualitative judgement, like an application essay and the particular after-school activities a student might have been involved in (and what each of those may be worth), and then there are the pieces of an application used for quantitative judgement, like test scores and their GPA. An application committee makes a quantitative judgement to decide if quantitative scores meet their expectations, and then takes a look at everything else. Is four years on the debate team equivalent to two years on the soccer team and two years in the art club? That's a qualitative judgement that can determine a lot.

Twilight of the Idols

Think about all of the qualitative and quantitative factors that go into deciding on how strong a single candidate or student is, and then multiply that by thousands to think about how you might judge a whole university. There's no simple way to do it. Sure, you can measure the prestige of a school by measuring median GPA and SAT schools of the incoming students who are accepted, but that tells us nothing about the quality of the actual education there.

I say this to make a specific point. At the University level, we lack reliable metrics to substantiate the quality of the education being received. Yes, we have peer review organizations of accreditation, both regional and national, but often each of these groups disagree with the standards of the others in large, sometimes very public, battles. What we lack is objective measurement(s). In lieu of that, those wealthy families send their children here not on the basis of certain educational quality, but on the basis of brand and reputation.; meanwhile, the measurable part of our education system continues to languish. Yes, like many of our idols, the brand is persisting while the reality has long since faded.

Therefore, we have to focus on what we do know, and what our tax dollars primarily fund—our K-12 educational system, which is what will end up determining our students' success in college. Here's what we know: across the board, our schools fall behind others around the world, displaying either near average or below average scores across science, mathematics, and reading. It's well-known that the Asian countries' schools tend to score more highly across the board (especially in math and science), but so, too, do most of the European countries' schools. Mostly notably, those of the Scandinavian countries.

How do we know? There are a variety of tests—PISA, TIMSS, and NAEP to name a few—that give the same questions, every three years, to a statistically significant number of students in each country in order to provide a comparison of current comprehension.

A fair counterargument you might hear is that standardized testing is a poor metric for assessing the quality of an education or the preparedness of students. On the whole I agree, for the record. But in a country where education is built around preparing students for standardized tests, it does become a dominant reflection on the quality of *that* education.

The problem with any argument that discounts our low-to-average test scores is that it tends to then become that our educational system is the best in the world, because we dominate the world's economy. We produce leaders and entrepreneurs like no one else, so our lower-than-average test scores don't matter. Except that isn't statistically true, either.

This is another idol we believe in that the numbers don't reflect. Yes, we dominate the world's economy, because of the prior wealth we've built, but what is the trend moving forward? The Organization for Economic Cooperation and Development (OECD) provides international research, offering side-by-side comparisons of entrepreneurship in different economies. The number of new businesses formed isn't important. The number of new businesses that go on to have paid employees is important. In OECD's 2013 research, if we look at new businesses that create jobs, we see that our nation had the second-lowest rate of the twenty-five Western economies measured.[62] New businesses are on the decline in terms of overall job creation, and a growing number of businesses, now over 20 percent, are built out of a lack of employment to be found elsewhere. So, yes, we have a lot of new businesses forming, but they're formed out of desperation and they aren't creating jobs. The number of new businesses filed is a completely false metric by which to claim entrepreneurship is thriving in our country. The right metric is the number of jobs these companies are creating, the real income and size of our middle class and, finally, how many of our citizens can afford

---

62 Jordan Weissman, "Think We're the Most Entrepreneurial Country in the World? Not So Fast," *The Atlantic,* last modified October 2, 2012, https://www.theatlantic.com/business/archive/2012/10/think-were-the-most-entrepreneurial-country-in-the-world-not-so-fast/263102/.

essential living expenses like homes, food, clothes, a car, and an education for their children.

I'll say that again. We claim entrepreneurship is healthy in this country because new businesses are being formed. Yet, data really show that these new businesses don't go on to create jobs and that a significant portion are being formed in desperation for a lack of economic opportunity. This is very much like claiming our economy is strong because stock prices are up when fewer and fewer Americans are able to afford stocks. It sounds good as a political sound bite, but only serves to further isolate and shame real Americans who live with the economic reality.

Our economy already feels the consequence of this path. As we talk about the "skill gap," what we're really struggling to address is the growing number of people who are not properly trained for today's economy. Yes, there are some industries that pay well and are having job shortages, but that is not a reflection of most of the economy.

Most Millennials will have a lower socioeconomic standing than their parents. That's the overall economic reality. Far more will find themselves in the "gig economy" than in the few fields with stable, well-paying jobs. So, when people argue our education is the best in the world because our economy is the best in the world, I'd say their view of our economy is based on wealth that was built generations ago and is now in rapid decline.

As a brief aside, if you want to push more students toward STEM fields, then you need to expose them in their early development far before picking their college programs. In order to increase our young students' access to and understanding of STEM fields, we should ensure our public universities offer college credit to graduate students in these STEM fields who will come assist our primary and secondary teachers in teaching STEM curriculum. In short, we need people passionate about STEM assisting K-12 teachers who don't have STEM backgrounds in sharing these fields with students at an earlier enough age to be impactful, which is a topic I've written about before.[63]

Back to the main point, you might be asking the question— what does an economic trend creating the first generation in American history to be worse off than their parents have to do with our education system? It's simply this: whenever someone in a political debate points out how much our child's education is falling behind, the counterargument is made that we have the strongest economy in the world. If other countries are doing a better job preparing their next generation, then why are we winning economically?

I'm here to say this red herring is based on a ghost. The economic engine that will define the fate of our economy in the years to come is completely and entirely different than it was when it created the economy we have enjoyed over the last thirty years. If we want the next thirty years to look anything like the last thirty, then it's time to face that head-on and do something about it. Otherwise, it's just a matter of time until the reality catches up to us. Our economy *is* indicating that our educational system is broken.

In fact, our education system can play a role in fixing our economy if we shift our focus from comprehension to critical thinking, and from employment to entrepreneurship. And that means taking a serious look at how standardized testing is itself failing our society. This is one of the most powerful moves we could make to get the economy back on track. In lieu of having jobs available, we should be teaching as many students as possible how to create them for themselves and others. To tap into that rugged spirit of self-reliance and commitment to building community once again.

There is a long tradition of standardized testing, both globally and in the United States. However, it has only recently

---

63 Alex Berezow and Brayden Olson, "Let Grad Students Teach Science to Kids: Column," *USA Today*, last modified September 7, 2016, https://www.usatoday.com/story/opinion/2016/09/07/education-science-elementary-schools-graduate-students-teachers-column/89884940/.

become the monster we know it as today. The earliest record of standardized testing is from the 1st century Hans dynasty in China, where individuals looking for jobs in government were tested on their knowledge of philosophy and poetry, while in the West, we favored essays to determine a candidate's knowledge. This practice stemmed from the Socratic method of teaching. However, as our system grew, we looked for more quantitative methods of judging an individual's knowledge and preparedness. Initially, this was just addressed with the SAT to help colleges with their admissions process, but that began expanding into other tests. Then, in 2001, with No Child Left Behind, we created a system where most students are assessed every year in the most quantitative way possible—as a means of assessing their school's performance.

The unintended consequence is that, rather than improving the quality of our schools and education, we have shifted to a model of preparing students to take tests. Like many shortcomings we see in policy and legislation, standardized testing is related to money in politics. Four of the top corporations in the standardized testing market, Pearson Education, ETS (Educational Testing Service), Houghton Mifflin Harcourt, and McGraw-Hill collectively spent more than $20 million through their lobby efforts from 2009 to 2014. This lobbying helps fuel an industry that's worth nearly $2 billion a year.[64]

For fear of their schools or their careers negatively affected by low test scores, teachers and administrators are forced to prioritize teaching students how to ace tests—*teaching to the tests* rather than *to the students*—and the quality of an education is of lower priority than the fact that most students score well on the test. In fact, this obsession has driven school administrators to simply cheat on these tests to inflate the test scores, a practice

---

64 Valerie Strauss, "Report: Big Education Firms Spend Millions Lobbying for Pro-testing Policies," *The Washington Post,* last modified March 30, 2015, https://www.washingtonpost.com/news/answer-sheet/wp/2015/03/30/report-big-education-firms-spend-millions-lobbying-for-pro-testing-policies/?utm_term=.dbe0938ff579.

made infamous in Atlanta where forty-four out of fifty-six schools were recently found to have cheated.[65] That is how important the tests have become. Whether the students retain the knowledge, or understand how it all fits together…well, there's just not really time to worry about that.

I will argue that we absolutely should move away from teaching to the tests, but beyond that there is more we can do to improve our system. We need to offer more incentives, including debt forgiveness for student loans, to encourage the best of us to pursue teaching. We need to make the career track of being a teacher more attractive, rather than allow it to continue being a path known for long hours, hard work, and low pay. Recently, we've seen large scale, organized teacher protests in Arizona, Colorado, Kentucky, Oklahoma, and West Virginia. The Economic Policy Institution reports that, adjusted for inflation, teachers actually make less in 2016 than almost two decades earlier while, as we know, the adjusted cost of everything from housing to food has gone up.[66] And, that is only the tip of the iceberg. Schools struggle to fund textbooks, transportation, or professional development for teachers. Let alone mental health and counseling services. We also need to get technology into the classroom so that it can support our best teachers and their curriculum. For instance, while more than sixty-five studies have definitively proven that interactive video games lead to better knowledge training, skill training, and overall retention of learning, it still is virtually non-existent in our K-12 education.[67] So, our teachers are not only

65   Elizabeth Flock, "APS (Atlanta Public Schools) Embroiled in Cheating Scandal," *The Washington Post,* last modified July 2011, https://www.washingtonpost.com/blogs/blogpost/post/aps-atlanta-public-schools-embroiled-in-cheating-scandal/2011/07/11/gIQAJl9m8H_blog.html?utm_term=.6a28127a73fd.

66   Katherine Barrett and Richard Greene, "The Real Reason Behind Recent Teacher Strikes – and Why They're Likely to Continue," *Governing,* last modified May 10, 2018, http://www.governing.com/topics/mgmt/gov-real-reason-teacher-strikes-continue.html.

67   David Kelly, "Study Shows Employees Learn Best from Video Games," University of Colorado Denver, last modified October 19, 2010, https://www.cudenvertoday.org/videogamesmakebetteremployees/.

struggling financially, they lack the infrastructure necessary to do their job, know better tools are available that they can't access, and spend their lives prepping students for tests rather than teaching. It's no wonder this isn't working.

We need teachers to make enough to survive. We need schools to be able to afford critical infrastructure *and* the best educational tools available. But, most importantly, we need to move beyond teaching to the test so that teachers can be allowed to teach students course material that prepares them for this century-- because that is why they decided to be a teacher in the first place. They know it's not about knowing information off the top of your head, but learning how to better process and critically think through that information. We're preventing our teachers from really doing what they want to be doing, which is truly teaching the next generation what they need to know.

So, what is beyond the test? In order to answer that, we have to get on the same page in understanding that there are two reasons we currently test students: college admittance and assessing the quality of our schools.

For colleges and universities, we have to recognize that we are moving toward a new kind of economy. If colleges would allow examinations relevant to a field of study (for instance, engineering or business examinations to address a student's level of knowledge), then students could specialize earlier in their education. This would pave the way to allow students and teachers to focus on a learner's strengths, since college admission would be tied to specific career skills; it could also open the door to more people studying for only two years in a career they are certain they want to pursue, rather than two years of more general electives. In an economy where more and more people are struggling to afford a four-year education, this could be a godsend. In fact, in many European countries three-year college degrees are commonplace. For students who are placed directly into a specialized program, two-year degrees could be absolutely attainable, covering almost all the same career-relevant coursework we currently teach in four-year programs.

Does this mean I'm against general education as a whole? No, some people benefit tremendously from it. Heck, I'd value exposing more students to philosophy in their education, but that simply isn't for everyone. We shouldn't be forcing everyone down a path of fifteen or more years of general education when many are ready to specialize earlier and others are forced to take on education and debt they don't want and can't afford.

It would also work against a trend where students who take college-level courses in high-school or community college, and then transfer into universities, have to retake classes within their discipline or area of study, which can also happen when a student transfers from one university to another. In other words, transfer students are often forced to retake classes no matter how well they did the first time, sometimes adding whole semesters to their educational years, and often adding significant cost by discouraging students from beginning at a more affordable community college and then transferring to a big-name university. If anything, we should legislatively support the transition from community college to big-name university as much as possible, because of the radical impact it could have on reducing the cost of education for lower income households, while giving them access to the same opportunities as children from other economic backgrounds. For instance, programs like Running Start here in Washington State, which subsidize student tuition at local community colleges for students with high grade performance, should be expanded and promoted nationally. I, myself, am a graduate from Running Start.

For primary school, we need to make the testing longitudinal, tracking students over a longer period of time. Rather than examining a student in a particular moment of their education, we need to look at how it supports them in moving forward. How are students performing on their college admission exams? How are they performing in the job market? Are they able to get jobs and succeed on a professional level?

Essentially, I'm arguing that we should measure schools

against what they're supposed to produce: productive, successful humans, capable of critical thinking.

Right now, we fund schools based on performance for end-of-year standardized tests, but measuring schools by whether or not they're meeting our societal expectations for education is possible. Today's technology allows us to easily track this data over time to see where students from a given school end up as an aggregate, big group. I don't mean a one-off research study. I mean anonymously tracking student data throughout their career to see which students end up in which colleges or which income brackets. While we wouldn't know which student is which, we would see which schools that individual has attended and through large enough data sets, watch these trends.

Coming from an education family, let me be clear I know students step into the classroom with wildly different resources, capabilities, access, and likely life outcomes. My mother, who teaches 3rd and 4th grade, has always picked schools with high rates of free and reduced lunch, because that is where teaching can be the hardest and most rewarding. I know a teacher can only do so much for children who don't have the same opportunity at home as other students. So, to be clear, in the model above we could easily track outcomes based on expected performance and evaluate schools and teachers on a fair and equitable playing field, without penalizing those who choose to serve in the most challenging way possible.

In the business world, the value of big data in showing us these kinds of patterns, transforming our decisions and changing the world. This shift would free up administrators, teachers, and students to focus on the kind of education that really prepares them for the real world, and puts the focus on life outcomes not scores.

Have you asked your kids how they feel about standardized tests? Have you asked any of their teachers in a forum where they felt comfortable giving you an honest answer? I bet I know what virtually every teacher and student would say. And if you still need one more reason for this shift, just think about your own career. How many standardized tests have you had to take since you got your current job? Are your future raises or promotions going to be based off of your ability to take a test well? If not, then why have students spend eighteen years getting good at this skill?

If we want to tie funding to performance, we should be attaching it to long-term performance. You'd see curricula change overnight to focus on preparing students for celebrating their strengths rather than mitigating their weaknesses. There'd be a focus on critical thinking and overall understanding, rather than on short-term memorization of facts and how to take tests.

This would immediately shift the focus from acquiring the skill of being good at taking tests to acquiring the ability to think critically and succeed in the real world. Our teachers would be the first to celebrate this change.

While we are on the topic of schools, I want to make one final comment that is once again at the center of public consciousness in the United States right now. Gun violence in schools. The right rallies around the Second Amendment. The left around legislating our way out of the problem. This is yet another issue where partisanship has led to more distraction and attempts to score political points than real solutions.

In most cases, the parent legally obtained the weapon and would continue to do so under any legislation we put in place. The student then illegally obtains the weapon from the parents. Attempting to fix gun violence by legislation is like trying to end the *demand* for drugs by increasing criminalization on drug dealers.

The second common element throughout every school shooting is that the offender needed mental health support. If we want to reduce the amount of gun violence in our schools, then we need to further fund mental health services throughout our public school systems and our population in general. We need to get more staff on hand that can identify and support at-risk youth before they become violent. It's a bi-partisan answer that could provide a real solution.

Chapter 4

Greatness Measured by the Treatment
of our Weakest Citizens

"The moral test of government is how that government treats those who are in the dawn of life, the children; those who are in the twilight of life, the elderly; those who are in the shadows of life; the sick, the needy and the handicapped."

—Vice President Hubert Humphrey, 1977.

When we explore the landscape of economic inequality and ask where it is that a struggling family is finally crushed by poverty, we most often find unplanned illness and medical expenses. As CNN and Kaiser Family Foundation have famously reported, the number one cause of bankruptcy is medical expenses.[68] [69]

If economic inequality is the undercurrent behind all the issues we're discussing in this book, health care is the wave crashing onto the beach. It's the economic issue garnering the most political attention at the moment, as left and right fight over the *if* and *how*.

---

68 Dan Mangan, "Medical Bills Are the Biggest Cause of US Bankruptcies: Study," *CNBC*, last modified July 24, 2013, https://www.cnbc.com/id/100840148.

69 Liz Hamel et al., "The Burden of Medical Debt: Results from the Kaiser Family Foundation/New York Times Medical Bills Survey," Kaiser Family Foundation, last modified January 5, 2016, https://www.kff.org/report-section/the-burden-of-medical-debt-section-3-consequences-of-medical-bill-problems/.

As such, debate rages about whether we should attribute these bankruptcies to medical costs or all the debts and expenses the American was under before the illness.[70] This argument, about the mounting debt across the board, only further stresses the key point of this book: that these issues are inextricably tied by the changing economic paradigm toward further consolidation.

We stand alone in the developed world as the only country out of the fifty most developed countries without universal health care.[71] It's the most basic of equities, of rights, in a developed world, but our commitment to economic consolidation (or companies running Congress)—rather than to morality or fiscal conservatism—is keeping universal health care from being built into the fabric of our society.

In this chapter, I'll be tackling the issues, statistics, and research on both sides to show why those committed to fiscal conservatism and social equality both want the same plan—and neither party is offering it.

No matter which side of this debate you are on, I think few disagree that we have a serious problem in our current form.

I'm talking about men and women who forego screening and treatment because they can't afford insurance, only to see their medical condition and suffering escalate right along with the eventual medical treatments.[72] Cancers that may have been treatable are left unchecked until the outcome is near certain and the costs are beyond measure.

---

70 Megan McArdle, "The Truth about Medical Bankruptcies," *The Washington Post,* last modified March 26, 2018, https://www.washingtonpost.com/blogs/post-partisan/wp/2018/03/26/the-truth-about-medical-bankruptcies/?utm_term=.b6f31fae1207.

71 Thomas DeMichele, "The U.S. Is the Only Very Highly Developed Country without Universal HealthCare," Fact / Myth, last modified March 13, 2018, http://factmyth.com/factoids/the-us-is-the-only-very-highly-developed-country-without-universal-healthcare/.

72 Dhruv Khullar, "As a Doctor, I See How a Lack of Health Insurance Worsens Illness and Suffering," *The Washington Post,* last modified January 9, 2017, https://www.washingtonpost.com/news/to-your-health/wp/2017/01/09/doctors-see-how-a-lack-of-health-insurance-exacerbates-illness-and-suffering/?utm_term=.73c5731b0e5b.

Twilight of the Idols

I'm talking about men and women who choose to die—quietly and painfully—because they can't reasonably afford any treatment, and choosing to submit to death seems like a better option than leading their family to bankruptcy. I'm talking about men and women who succumb to their illnesses in a one-bedroom apartment, surrounded by family members who understand that technology and science could have helped, if insurance had allowed for treatment, as did the Portillo family, who bravely shared their experience in an article with The Nation magazine about watching their father painfully die.[73] And I'm talking about parents who don't even bother going to a doctor to take care of their own health or illnesses because they're afraid that doing so will make it impossible for them to pay the rent, buy food for their children, or keep their jobs.

And, in all actuality, I'm not only talking about those who have no health insurance at all. There are also countless individuals who struggle to pay for insurance that, in the end, still leaves them with debilitating debt from health care because it has covered only a fraction of their costs. Still others are left arguing with the insurance companies they've paid thousands of dollars to, stuck in between their doctors and their insurers on endless phone calls. Do you know someone who was forced out of treatment early because their insurance refused to cover the time that a hospital or doctor said was necessary? Or someone who put off treatment for an injury or illness for so long that, in the end, they were in debilitating pain and the problem was untreatable, or had caused far more pain and heartache than it should have? Chances are, you do. Maybe you've even been in this position yourself.

If we are to call ourselves a great nation with any seriousness at all, we have to do better by these families. And, to speak clearly and across economic and political boundaries, helping

---

73 Mark Betancourt, "The Devastating Process of Dying in America without Insurance," *The Nation,* last modified June 20, 2016, https://www.thenation.com/article/the-devastating-process-of-dying-in-america-without-insurance/.

these families when illness can be prevented will save billions of taxpayer dollars, which I'll discuss shortly.

We talk about the number of people who are uninsured in our country. We talk about these raw, massive numbers—like the twenty-eight million Americans who were without coverage in 2016. We talk about statistics, noting that repealing the Affordable Care Act (ACA) will leave another eighteen million people without coverage immediately. And fourteen million more by 2026.[74]

It's easy to see these as just numbers, unless you're living in a working-class family; then it can mean watching your father suffer in a body riddled by tumors and sores without so much as pain medication as happened to the Portillo family[75]. The Commonwealth Fund has helped chronicle more than a hundred such interviews to share the human side of the story, but these numbers are, again, in the tens of millions.[76]

The truth is, when we talk about it in terms of statistics it is easy to see why there is such a debate. Especially when the debate happens between members of Congress whose medical access for their families won't be impacted regardless of the outcome. On the whole, Congress is wealthier than ever, in fact, and gaining wealth much faster than the people they're representing.[77]

But if you can't afford health care or health insurance, all of the things that can go wrong on a daily basis are in front of you at every moment—they're very real worries, and you know just what it will mean if you get sick or find yourself injured.

---

74 Jessie Hellmann, "CBO: 18 Million Could Lose Coverage after ObamaCare Repeal," *The Hill*, last modified January 17, 2017, http://thehill.com/policy/healthcare/314549-study-obamacare-repeal-could-leave-32-million-without-coverage.

75 Betancourt, "The Devastating Process of Dying in America without Insurance."

76 Susan Sered, "Uninsured Americans Tell Their Stories," The Commonwealth Fund, accessed November 29, 2018, https://www.commonwealthfund.org/publications/publication/uninsured-americans-tell-their-stories.

77 David Hawkings, "Wealth of Congress: Richer than Ever, but Mostly at the Very Top," *Roll Call*, last modified February 27, 2018, https://www.rollcall.com/news/hawkings/congress-richer-ever-mostly-top.

The worst part is that there is nothing to oppose here in this debate.

Generally, the debate is that while ideal, we simply cannot afford something like the ACA, much less universal or single-payer health care. You'll hear things like, *these are pipedreams that might work in other countries with other structures, but they simply don't economically work here. We're already in crippling debt and the only path forward will require reducing the national deficit as it is.*

Those who are dedicated above all else to fiscal conservatism should be some of the strongest universal health care advocates. Why? Because the fiscally responsible decision is also the moral decision. In fact, experiments by companies in the private sector are already providing the research the public sector needs to recognize universal health care is the fiscally responsible choice. Analysis has shown that the more we invest in prevention, the more we save in treatment. To be specific, *Health Affairs*, the leading journal of health policy thought and research, published findings in 2010 to attest to the fact that for every dollar spent in prevention, organizations saved $3.27 on subsequent medical costs and $2.73 on absentee costs to businesses. Simply put, we could spend one dollar instead of six.[78]

What most people don't realize is that U.S. taxpayers and businesses are already funding a more expensive version of universal health care—we're just doing it in the emergency rooms, and often when it is too late. Consider the case of someone who can't afford yearly physical exams, and doesn't feel they can afford even a basic trip to a doctor's office. They put off a small pain or warning sign, avoiding what might have been a single visit to a doctor's office and a single shot, a round of treatment, a lifestyle change, or a more minor surgery. Over time, the pain or disease becomes unbearable, and suddenly they're in the emergency

---

78 Katherine Baicker, David Cutler, and Zirui Song, "Workplace Wellness Programs Can Generate Savings," *Health Affairs* 29, no. 2 (2010), last modified February 1, 2010, https://www.healthaffairs.org/doi/10.1377/hlthaff.2009.0626.

room, racking up tens of thousands of dollars in costs that could have been prevented.

Now, if this isn't something you've witnessed, you might think it's a crazy example. You might think, *Well, they're stupid—they should have gone to the doctor to begin with so that that didn't happen. That has to be rare.* In fact, it isn't. The National Institute of Health conducted research in 2014 to conclude that a third of those failing to seek medical care did so because of high cost or no health insurance.[79]

These are families who had to prioritize rent, food, or education for their children, gas for work. These people aren't stupid. They aren't avoiding medical help. They're being forced to prioritize food, shelter, their children, and health care.

Now, speaking to my fellow business owners and capitalists out there, this isn't just wrecking lives and families. It's ruining lives and costing taxpayers more money. We pay it in the emergency rooms rather than the doctor's office, but we pay three times as much as we would for prevention alone.

A strong counterargument you're likely to hear is that the ACA is absolutely *not* fiscally conservative. As the ACA may or may not be reversed, changed, or repealed, I will expand on this health care plan broadly supported by the Democratic Party—by whatever name you we call it. You might say that it increases health care costs, raises insurance premiums, and adds to taxes and adds to debt. Well, to you, I say... yes. Absolutely, you're exactly right. The objective of the left is access. The objective of the right is low cost. Neither is proposing the right solution or addressing the real issue that could lead to access and lower costs. Neither party is proposing a solution that would tackle the root cause: the oligopoly of health care giants who fund their campaigns.

I'll quote *Health Affairs* again; also in 2010, they reported health care costs were going up, premiums were going up, and a

---

79 Jennifer M. Taber, Bryan Leyva, and Alexander Persoskie, "Why Do People Avoid Medical Care? A Qualitative Study Using National Data," *Journal of General Internal Medicine* 30, no. 3 (2014): 290-7, last modified November 12, 2014, https://www.ncbi.nlm.nih.gov/pmc/articles/PMC4351276/.

bulk of that expense was shouldered by the workers right after the ACA (or ObamaCare.)[80]

That's right: the leading journal on health policy and research published a report stating that the ACA was going to increase all of our costs at the same time that they published findings to show that we can massively save by investing in prevention and access to health care a few months earlier.

How is that possible? That's what happens when you allow oligopolies and monopolies to form.

I'll stress the point even further. In a private, candid moment after a significant issue with my insurer, my own doctor's office encouraged me to go without health insurance. Given my age, health, and the cost of my premiums, even with the penalties I would have to pay, I would come out way ahead.

It varies from insurer to insurer, but medical professionals encounter such a high level of complications when working with them that they are willing to charge 50 percent less to be paid directly. They all have to add in a 50 percent premium for those with medical insurance, because the insurers are so hard to work with that doctors charge different rates for the same procedures, depending on what an administrative or bureaucratic nightmare the insurer presents. That should make any fiscal conservative scream.

Affordability and accessibility are two different things. The terms are confused in current political vernacular, partly because we call the ACA the *Affordable* Care Act; but this law wasn't put in place to make things more affordable—it was put in place to make sure that health care is more accessible, given that it requires that people get health care insurance and guarantees that people will not be turned down because of pre-existing conditions that, without a doubt, might have kept them from getting health care in the past. So, more people have health care, but it's more expensive

---

80 Gary Claxton et al., "Health Benefits in 2010: Premiums Rise Modestly, Workers Pay More toward Coverage," *Health Affairs* 29, no. 10 (2010), last modified October 1, 2010, https://www.healthaffairs.org/doi/10.1377/hlthaff.2010.0725.

overall and more expensive on the worker than it was before. It's just easier to get, and you can't live in denial that you'll ever get sick. It would be nice, and a lot of people were choosing that option of denial until the ACA passed, but, realistically, you need to face it now if you haven't faced it before: at some point, you will need to take advantage of this country's health care system—its doctors, technology, and medicine.

In order to make health care and health insurance affordable (in other words, actually cost our government *and* the insured less), we would have to go after the health care insurance companies. We'd have to break up the oligopoly. The free market would drive down inefficiency, bureaucracy, and profit margins and push organizations to adopt technology that would decrease costs.

Let's take one specific example. If there was a new entrant in the market that made it vastly easier for my doctor and others so that they no longer needed to charge the 50 percent premium, how much could be saved on infrastructure that neither the doctor or patient even want?

Why is our health care system so fiscally irresponsible?

Almost 15 percent of our health care costs are "administrative" costs, which is far higher than that of any other country. The quintessential example is Duke University Hospital, which has 1,300 billing clerks and only 900 patient beds.[81] In an environment of free market competition this couldn't stand. The competitive market would reduce these costs and push market share (and profits) to the most efficient and effective organizations. Only oligopolies and monopolies can thrive when both their customers and business partners pay more and get less than what they want.

We also lead the world in the amount of money we have to spend on "defensive medicine." Defensive medicine accounts for costs associated purely with protecting against lawsuits, is

---

81 David Cutler, "Why Does Health Care Cost So Much in America? Ask Harvard's David Cutler," PBS, last modified November 19, 2013, https://www.pbs.org/newshour/economy/why-does-health-care-cost-so-m.

estimated to cost us $650–$850 billion a year,[82] and it is caused by doctors being legally required (by some of those administrators and their own insurance) to unnecessarily re-order tests or order additional tests, even when a diagnosis is already certain. It's like when you watch a football replay ten times, just to take up on-air time, when everyone has already seen it and saw it again. Maybe you need one extra replay to be sure. But then not the seven more after that. In football, this costs a minute of your time, but in medicine it is costing over a half trillion dollars a year.

And, once more, we lead the world in supporting an irrationally high cost of drugs. Quite frankly, we need to set all U.S. drug prices at the same rates that we sell these same drugs in Europe and other stable markets. In fact, the top twenty best-selling medicines are three times cheaper in Europe.[83]

Most people believe the supply chain of their prescription involves a drug manufacturer, their doctor, and their pharmacist. However, a little known, but powerful entity in prescription drug distribution and pricing is known as a Pharmacy Benefit Manager. What do these entities do? Buy in bulk, markup, and re-sell to more than 50 percent of pharmacy clients—and most Americans have never even heard of them. Yet, it's prescription-buying Americans who, quite literally, foot the additional bill. In a market with healthy competition, these kinds of costs would be eliminated, too.

As a quick divergence, our litigious legal system is an entirely separate and noteworthy problem that's involved in this mess. The United States has just 4 percent of the world's population, yet we have 80 percent of the *world's lawyer population*. That's right, more lawyers than the rest of the world combined, and then

---

82 "Physician Study: Quantifying the Cost of Defensive Medicine," Jackson Healthcare, last modified February 2010, https://jacksonhealthcare.com/media-room/surveys/defensive-medicine-study-2010/.

83 Ben Hirschler, "How the U.S. Pays 3 times More for Drugs," *Scientific American*, accessed November 29, 2018, https://www.scientificamerican.com/article/how-the-u-s-pays-3-times-more-for-drugs/.

some.[84] That means there are a lot of lawyers out there who are actively looking for cases, and by extension, looking for people to blame for problems. Since hospitals and doctors can be big ticket items, they become common targets. 75 percent of these medical malpractice claims don't succeed, but lawyers still do well when just one in four do. In most other legal systems, the loser must pay a portion of the winner's legal fees. If law firms had to do the same here, you'd see far fewer frivolous malpractice claims and much lower costs of medicine.

So, what is happening in our health care system? We have a handful of all-powerful organizations that have organized our system and our medicine to ensure their well-being at the expense of everyone else's well-being. We've let regional and national oligopolies form—creating a system with a very small amount of competition—and the system's power is reinforced because it's not as if we can say we don't need a health care system. Depending on where you live, you have a handful of insurance choices names like Kaiser, United Health, Humana, Aetna, Blue Cross. You also have regional health care providers that probably only take these select insurances.

There are ways to fix this, much as politicians and the system itself have led you to believe otherwise. As a people, we need to take on big pharma and insurance. We need to use anti-trust to take on big insurers so that their surviving entities and smaller companies can compete at lower prices. We need to require that any medicine with life-saving implications be made accessible to everyone who needs it, or else we need to rescind the medicines' patents so that generics can come to market and make it affordable.

And we can do this, but right now we have a broken system, and implementing small fixes isn't doing us any good.

We're fighting about how to make medicine accessible or make it affordable when this is a false choice to begin with. The correct

---

84 "Sue-Happy America," eLocal Legal Resource Network, last modified September 7, 2011, https://www.elocal.com/content/legal-resource-network/sue-happy-america-2115.

answer is that we address the problem of an uncompetitive market, rather than tackling either the symptom of unaffordability or the symptom of lack of access. We're driving our country and our families into massive debt, which by all accounts has become the primary cause of bankruptcy, while simultaneously not providing universal health care to our most vulnerable citizens. There's no reason at all for us to be doing so, unless you're one of the very few who happens to be getting rich off of the system. It's a safe bet that you're not. Right now, everyone loses so that a small handful of organizations can win big. Even those who provide the care lose in this system. If we fix things, we'll all benefit, and we'll also be saving years of pain and heartache that will otherwise torment the weakest among us.

Simply put, Americans on the right and the left have a clear path to come together in political unity over this issue, just like every other modernized country in the world has done. This shouldn't be a partisan argument, or require any debate at all. It's not about repealing or keeping the ACA. Instead, it's about anti-trust legislation—breaking up the oligopoly in medical insurance and drug production to allow the free market to solve our problem. Then, from that position, we could actually propose legislating a universal health care plan that could give everyone access, reduce our costs, and preserve a competitive marketplace all at the same time.

Universal health care is a conservative issue, and it's also a liberal issue. And, as much as anything, it's a moral issue and a common sense one. It will reduce taxes. It will reduce the deficit. It will improve business performance. And, it will save lives.

Chapter 5

The Greatest Middle Class in the World

It was the dawn of a new era. The United States became the envy of the world after World War II, and it seemed like we had it all. Just about anyone with a high school diploma could look forward to a job that paid enough to support a family. Every modern convenience, two cars in every garage, and a house with a white picket fence.

Our economy was booming. Our future was bright. Many of us still think back to this time as the iconic Golden Age of American Society. Movies and television shows idealize this era as the "Happy Days."

But, what was so good about this time? And, what changed it? Simply put, this was the era when the United States achieved the lowest levels of inequality in recorded history,[85] and that translated into a middle class that more of us could participate in.

After World War II, once our soldiers came back from war, more of us really did "have it all" than at any time since. Of course, not everyone benefited. The Civil Rights movement hadn't really begun, and African-Americans were far less likely to share in this American dream. But, those who were our middle class were far better off than the majority of middle-class Americans today.

---

85 "Income Inequality in the United States," Inequality.org, accessed November 29, 2018, https://inequality.org/facts/income-inequality/.

Twilight of the Idols

Think about what you know of history, and the way your parents or grandparents lived. Right now, there's a good chance that your family has a fair amount of debt, not enough money in savings, and very real concerns about the future when it comes to how to pay for medical expenses, pay off debt, or get the youngest members of your family on solid footing for their own futures—through college or any other path. To get specific, debt for those aged 25-34 has now reached over $40,000 meaning debt for the average young family is above $80,000.[86]

These kind of facts are often rebuked with arguments like the strength of our overall economy compared to other countries, or stocks being up, or unemployment being low. None of this is mutually exclusive in an economy committed to inequality. An economy committed to such extreme inequality could reach any amount of wealth without most of its citizenry seeing any benefit. We are making more money—but more people are struggling, fewer Americans are able to participate in the stock market, and unemployment is low, though people flock to jobs that can't pay their bills, which sends them further into debt.

The issue isn't the strength of the economy. It's how we organize it.

Globally, comparisons of the middle class are equally uninformed. Yes, globally the middle class is defined as the group of people who make just $10-20 per day.[87] In some countries, $100 a day can buy all of your meals, pay the mortgage on a mansion, and afford you a personal assistant who can bring you a latte promptly at 8 a.m. each morning. But in Seattle, for example, $100

---

86 Megan Leonhardt, "Millennials Ages 25–34 Have $42,000 in Debt, and Most of It Isn't from Student Loans," *CNBC*, last modified August 16, 2018, https://www.cnbc.com/2018/08/15/millennials-have-42000-in-debt.html.

87 Rakesh Kochhar, "Are You in the Global Middle Class? Find Out with Our Income Calculator," Pew Research Center, last modified July 16, 2016, http://www.pewresearch.org/fact-tank/2015/07/16/are-you-in-the-global-middle-class-find-out-with-our-income-calculator/.

a day would put you in the "extremely low-income" bracket.[88] You would likely struggle to pay for food and a one-bedroom studio, living every moment of every day worried about debt; you might well be more than willing to *take* a part-time job where you'd be expected to bring someone a latte promptly at 8 a.m. each morning just to have some additional income.

It's not the number of dollars you make that matters. It's what those dollars can buy where you live.

Only one fact matters: how many of your citizens can afford the basic, necessary cost of living without mounting ever greater debt? You can build the strongest economy in the world multiple times over, but so long as the rules of the game remain as they are, we will only see most Americans fall further into debt, desperation, and hopelessness. Eventually, the economy we want to defend will collapse in our time.

That's the problem in a nutshell, but this issue is far too easy to spin.

The thing is, it's easy to *say* the American middle class is better off than the rest of the world, because our median income *is* higher, and, for the most part, our middle class has gotten very good at promoting the illusion that we *are* doing well. In reality, we're not doing nearly so well as we'd like to think, and we're basing much of our optimism, to the extent that we still have it, on nostalgia for what we know America's middle class had a few generations back. That is the appeal of slogans like *Make America Great Again*. Yet, under the surface a super majority of the families voting for this hope will live and die in debt they can never repay.

The real questions are: Is it possible for these middle-class families to be self-sufficient while still affording education and medicine? And, will life be better for their children than it was for them, as it has been for all American generations until now? That is the benchmark of success. Is quality of life improving for our

---

88   Ryan Takeo, "$72,000 Considered 'Low Income' in King, Snohomish Counties for Family of Four," *King 5 News*, last modified April 26, 2017, http://www.king5.com/article/news/local/72000-considered-low-income-in-king-snohomish-counties-for-family-of-four/281-434107397.

children? Whether you're a Democrat or a Republican, you would be insane to think the answer to that question today is *yes*; both parties have contributed to the inequality during my lifetime.

U.S. News, in conjunction with Y&R's BAV Group and The Wharton School of the University of Pennsylvania, ranks the world's major countries on "quality of life," considering factors such as wealth, health, equality, global influence, and taxes. By those measures, the United States ranks No. 17 in the world, well behind leaders like Canada, Sweden, and Australia—and just ahead of No. 21 China. [89]

Compare the wealth of the top 5 percent to the median wealth of a country, and you'll see the United States is leading the world by more than *double* in having the most inequitable middle class of any country we measure in the OECD.[90] We have gone from leading the world in the 1950s to trailing the world today compared to all but the least capitalistic, most corrupt governments in the world.

Over the past fifty years, our country has seen some amazing changes when it comes to civil rights, science, and technology. The Internet informs us in ways we never were before. Smart phones allow us to connect with those we care about and stay safer than ever before. We have elected an African American president. In all of these arenas, we've grown incredibly, and surpassed what most of our grandparents could have imagined was possible for America's future generations. At the same time, our middle class has been allowed to shrink, day by day.

Only the most cynical member of the Greatest Generation would have ever imagined a world with these technological and scientific marvels beyond our wildest dreams, with more surplus than ever, within a society where our dystopian nightmares like *Ready Player One* and *Altered Carbon* are within grasp. No matter

---

89 Deidre McPhillips, "Quality of Life Rankings," *U.S. News & World Report,* last modified January 23, 2018, https://www.usnews.com/news/best-countries/quality-of-life-full-list.

90 "Global Inequality," Inequality.org, accessed November 29, 2018, https://inequality.org/facts/global-inequality/.

your politics, ask yourself, where do today's trends take us in twenty years?

We're not exaggerating when we say that in a 1950s household, a single income made ends meet so that one parent could stay at home to raise children, while another worked from 9 to 5 and came home for dinner. Yes, it's true that the glass ceiling and gender inequality pushed women to stay at home, and we've come a long way since then; the key thing to realize here is that the average household can no longer function in that same way. Not even if it wants to. If you're married, whether you're a man or a woman, there's a very good chance that one of you staying home from work would put a serious, if not fatal, strain on your finances. In the 1950s, dual-income households were less than 25 percent of the population. Today, they're more than 60 percent.[91] The issue here isn't having a dual-income family, but that there was a time in recent memory when our middle class was strong enough to cover all its living expenses on only one income.

Now? For most, even with twice the work hours in the household, they still live in debt. We have two-income households where two professional college graduates are struggling to pay their bills in such a fashion that the decision to have children is literally made because of the cost involved. There's simply no money to be spared, even though they have two full-time incomes and appear to be living a middle-class life. This has nothing to do with gender inequality. What I'm talking about here is the difference between a family of four being able to survive on a one-person income, in comparison to our society having reached a point where the average family of two or three requires two full-time incomes to manage the same quality of life, if not less. Our money is not going as far as it once did, and our costs are growing exponentially. Incomes have stagnated, while cost of living has skyrocketed due to inequality. Middle-class families now take on

---

91   "The Rise in Dual Income Households," Pew Research Center, last modified June 18, 2015, http://www.pewresearch.org/ft_dual-income-households-1960-2012-2/.

debt to fix a car, pay necessary medical expenses, or buy a child the computer they need if they want to do well in school.

Yes, every family still has a microwave and, for the most part, *also* has a home computer—if not multiple computers. Most families also have privately owned vehicles, a cable TV, and a washer and dryer. It is absolutely true that we have more things, but we've moved further away from having *everything* we need today. Sure, we have a microwave and an iPad, but we're also struggling to afford our cars, our education, and our health. In fact, we're struggling to pay for the homes that house those microwaves and computers.

So, what do we do? In the final chapter, I'll share how we get the kind of political representation to actually *do* the things I am about to propose, but for now I will stay focused on what we should do.

It's time to reduce the number of monopolies and oligopolies that are choking the life out of our small businesses in this country. Since 1996, we have seen the number of publicly traded companies in our country drop in half.[92] They've followed the same trends we've seen in our economy at large: fewer and fewer big winners. As an entrepreneur, I'll speak from personal experience to say if you're asked today how your company will make money for your shareholders, the only acceptable, credible answer is, "Be acquired." It's time for our leaders to take action to ensure a free market. This isn't a call for more regulation or less regulation. In some cases it is about more, in others it is about less, but only big business can afford lobbyists. So, it is a case of having representatives in office who will take actions to ensure a fair playing field for small business and do more than merely say, *small business is the backbone of the American economy.*

We also *must* stop treating our housing market as a commodity, period. It's not for investing and speculation. Houses are for people

---

92 Les Brorsen, "Looking behind the Declining Number of Public Companies," Harvard Law School, last modified May 18, 2017, https://corpgov.law.harvard.edu/2017/05/18/looking-behind-the-declining-number-of-public-companies/.

to live in and to slowly build economic security. We already have enough of an issue with our limited housing supply. We need to put legislation in place to keep speculators out of the real estate markets and increase supply to the point where local people can afford to build their futures. One such piece of legislation was recently passed in Vancouver, British Columbia to tax non-resident homeowners from buying properties to leave vacant or rent back to local residents. It was so successful, they have since expanded the tax.[93] Shortly after it passed, I spoke with dozens of legislators in Washington State from both parties, encouraging similar legislation to no avail, while articles circulated that almost half of our young people living in my area couldn't afford rent next year.[94] The most common pushback I received behind closed doors was, *Millennials don't vote and this won't look good for me politically.* As predicted, the non-resident home buyers flooded over from Vancouver, B.C. to Seattle.[95][96] And, the young people in our region who were already struggling saw the dream of homeownership move further out of reach.

This has been one of the most damning and obvious outcomes of economic inequality. Our next generation can't afford to transition into the middle class, continuously stuck in a cycle of rent and debt.

---

93   Natalie Obiko Pearson, "Vancouver's Hot Housing Market Gets Tougher for Wealthy Chinese," Bloomberg, last modified February 20, 2018, https://www.bloomberg.com/news/articles/2018-02-20/british-columbia-extends-housing-crackdown-with-tax-increases.

94   Mike Rosenberg, "Nearly Half of Local Millennials Consider Moving as Seattle-Area Home Costs Soar Again," *The Seattle Times,* last modified February 28, 2017, https://www.seattletimes.com/business/real-estate/nearly-half-of-local-millennials-consider-moving-as-seattle-area-home-costs-soar-again/.

95   Matt Phillips, "Chinese Money is Pouring into Seattle and Making Homes Crazy Expensive," *Vice Money,* last modified February 9, 2017, https://news.vice.com/en_us/article/j5d7e4/chinese-money-is-pouring-into-seattle-and-making-homes-crazy-expensive.

96   Ellen Sheng, "Seattle Real Estate Sees Surge in Chinese Interest after Vancouver Enacts 15% Tax," *Forbes,* last modified March 2, 2017, https://www.forbes.com/sites/ellensheng/2017/03/02/seattle-real-estate-sees-surge-in-chinese-interest-after-vancouver-enacts-15-tax/#35c51f8a65e1.

Twilight of the Idols

If we could make small business viable again, education affordable, and get our middle class back into homeownership, along with the other solutions discussed elsewhere in this book, we could start rebuilding a middle class for the world to envy.

Chapter 6

The Land of the Free

If you were to drive cross-country through the U.S., making small stops along the way to observe the cities, the countryside, the suburbs, and the ghost towns, you would get a glimpse of America. The shell of it. The literal *land of the free*.

You could peer out the window of your car and see those amber waves of grain blowing in a soft wind, or gaze out over the hills and valleys, relishing the dips and curves that create the landscape of our country, the pines that line the mountains, or the red dirt of the Ozark mountains. You'd recognize the bustling streets of Manhattan, or the quiet, almost lazy feel of the countryside, where the feel of the landscape contradicts all the hard work the people who live there put into maintaining that lazy feel—that easy, living ambiance which is so prominent in rural America that it may as well be trademarked and made exclusively ours.

There are parallels between the image of our country and those who reside within it. You do get a sense of freedom, traveling the open roads—there's a feeling that you could stop in any small town or massive city and just…start over. Begin afresh. And after you'd done so, the American Dream of prosperity and a wonderful sense of belonging to this great land of opportunity would be attainable. A land where one is free to pursue whatever lifestyle they may choose, be that the life of a Wall Street millionaire or the simple life of country living—waking up to the caws of the roosters and turning in for the night before the sun goes down so that you could wake up before the sun rose once again and get to work, maintaining and enjoying your simple life.

Diversity of lifestyle, culture, and even environment abounds in America, and that's one of the things that makes it great. Whether you want snow, beaches, mountains, plains, or even deserts, there's plenty of room for you to choose. It's a land of freedom, and we celebrate that just as we celebrate the opportunity that's meant to come along with it.

Yes, it's the land of the free, but not for all. Even at the lowest incarceration rate we have seen in two decades, we still incarcerate more people than any country in the world,[97] measured both in percentage and in total number. We have more than 25 percent more prisoners than China, even with their population being almost five times as large.[98]

Why? More than half of those in federal prison are there because of drugs or immigration (52.6 percent, at the time of writing).[99] Has this reduced the supply of drugs? The short answer is no.[100] [101] Rather, it has either negligible or non-existent effects other than increased potency, profit for sellers, and $30 billion spent per year in the U.S. And, nationally, more than 25 percent of

97   John Gramlich, "America's Incarceration Rate Is at a Two-Decade Low," Pew Research Center, last modified May 2, 2018, http://www.pewresearch.org/fact-tank/2018/05/02/americas-incarceration-rate-is-at-a-two-decade-low/.

98   "World Prison Populations," BBC News, accessed November 29, 2018, http://news.bbc.co.uk/2/shared/spl/hi/uk/06/prisons/html/nn2page1.stm.

99   "Offenses," Federal Bureau of Prisons, last modified October 27, 2018, https://www.bop.gov/about/statistics/statistics_inmate_offenses.jsp.

100   "World Drug Report 2015," United Nations Office on Drugs and Crime, accessed November 29, 2018, https://www.unodc.org/documents/wdr2015/World_Drug_Report_2015.pdf.

101   "Transnational Institute Progress Report as a Contribution to the Mid-Term (2003) Review of UNGASS," Transnational Institute, accessed November 30, 2018, https://www.tni.org/files/download/brief6.pdf.

the total prison population is considered to be made up of "non-violent, low-level offenders."[102]

But, in the land of the free, we're also all criminals. Yes, if only in some small way, all of us.

We have all committed an act within our lifetimes that would land us in trouble with the law, if not in prison. If you haven't driven under the influence, you've tried an illegal drug. If you haven't tried a drug, perhaps you drank as a minor. If you never drank while you were underage, perhaps you got overpaid on a paycheck once or expensed a work trip when you shouldn't have. At the very least, I bet you've gotten a speeding ticket, or gone over the speed limit without getting caught—either way, you broke the law. And if you don't have a car, and live in a city…well, are you really telling me you've never jaywalked or gone against a light that told you, in no uncertain terms, *Don't walk!*? The list goes on and on. Every single one of us has done something illegal, somewhere, at least once.

So, as we dive into a discussion of criminals, talking about those of us in America who are definitely not free, I encourage you to remember one of the most famous sayings out there: *Let he who is without sin cast the first stone.*

Those Americans who have spent time in prison have become altered due to this simple fact: they were simply unfortunate enough to be caught breaking a law which, in many cases, isn't so different from a law that you or your friends have broken in the past. You see, I'm not talking about the folks who are in prison for making choices that led to assault, rape, armed robbery, or other extreme acts that endangered the people around them.

There is, without doubt, a critical and important distinction we need to make. There is no question that certain broken laws must be punished with incarceration and nothing less, and the time in prison must be significant enough that it makes an impact.

---

102 Lauren-Brooke Eisen and Inimai Chettiar, "39% of Prisoners Should Not Be in Prison," *Time Magazine,* last modified December 9, 2016, http://time.com/4596081/incarceration-report/.

Murderers and rapists, among others, are groups of people who must be separated from society, as they *do* pose a dangerous threat to the residents of this country.

If you've been the victim of a violent attack, you deserve to have the peace of mind that comes with knowing your attacker has been put behind bars so that they cannot hurt you or anyone else again in the remotely near future. Let's get that straight before we go any further.

And yet, the crimes we've mentioned above aren't the average crimes.

We're talking about people who were growing marijuana in their backyard, who were in the country illegally or working illegally to take care of their families, or who got caught one too many times committing low-level criminal offenses. We're talking about immigrants who outstayed their visas, people who began growing marijuana on behalf of family members who could benefit from it medicinally, and individuals who were imprisoned for failing to meet some aspect of parole conditions because they needed work and found it across state lines. If we begin to talk about medicinal marijuana and marijuana use at all, regardless of where you stand on the topic of legalization, we also have to address the fact that our prison system is filled with people who've been imprisoned for something that's now been legalized in more than half of the country. We have men and women who are sitting behind bars for a decade's worth of time, as we speak, for doing something that many others now do legally and in the open. In fact, many are making millions of dollars a year selling marijuana professionally.

Yet, we spend billions in tax dollars to keep these people locked up, and many of our nation's prisons are for-profit institutions. That's not fiscally conservative at all.

Chances are, you and I have come to the same conclusion, and see evidence of a system that has gotten way out of hand.

It's worth keeping in mind that the number of prisoners in the U.S. makes up over *half* the number of prisoners worldwide, while we have only 4 percent of the world population; for every 100,000 residents, we incarcerate 737 people, whereas other first world countries tend to have incarceration rates well below that, at about one hundred prisoners per 100,000 residents.[103] You might be thinking that we're just tougher on crime. We're the "law and order" country. *You do the crime, you do the time; it's as simple as that.* But, is it really that simple?

We have more prisons than any other country in the world, and in most cases, we have them filled to the brim. Is it possible that the land of the free simply has many more "bad" people than any other country? One would certainly hope not, as that very notion would be contradictory to everything we claim to stand for. Not to mention the fact that, based on statistics, race and income level are directly related to how likely you are to go to prison for a crime. In fact, one in three African American men will spend time in prison, which is more than five times higher than the Caucasian incarceration rate. Yet, Caucasians are 45 percent more likely to sell and 25 percent more likely to use drugs.[104]

The truth is that America incarcerates people at alarming rates—and, by far and away, by more than two and a half times the rates for any other crime—for drug offenses, which have tripled in number since the 1980s.[105] We just arrest more often, for more offenses, and keep people in prison for longer.

Adding to our statistics is the fact that we have incredibly high rates of recidivism, which means that even once a man or woman gets out of jail, they are likely to go right back sooner than later. Some will probably argue that this is just a case of a leopard not being able to change its spots—once a criminal, always a criminal.

But I'm going to ask you to think about that for a minute.

---

103 "World Prison Populations."

104 Jonathan Rothwell, "How the War on Drugs Damages Black Social Mobility," Brookings, last modified September 30, 2014, https://www.brookings.edu/blog/social-mobility-memos/2014/09/30/how-the-war-on-drugs-damages-black-social-mobility/.

105 Michelle Alexander, *The New Jim Crow: Mass Incarceration in the Age of Colorblindness* (New York: New Press, 2010), 60.

Twilight of the Idols

Think about someone who goes to prison for, say, a month or two. They get sentenced to their time because of a first-time drug offense that's significant enough to put them in jail, but not significant enough to keep them there for any length of time. It's enough time, though, for them to realize their mistakes, and want to change.

The question is, what happens when they get out of jail? At best, they have someone to take them in—somewhere with a bed, food, and family or friends. At worst, they don't, and they end up looking for temporary room and board until they can *get their feet back under them*. Now, in the movies and on television, the problem of employment for men and women like this is given lip service. Life is shown to be difficult, but more often than not, somebody's willing to give them a chance. In the movies, in Hollywood, someone who's gone to prison for any length of time either gets out, finds a job, and turns over a new leaf; gets out and gets a job, but immediately proves to their supervisor that they should never have been given a chance; or, gets out and goes immediately back to a life of crime. In the movies and on television, it's generally that simple.

In real life, it's not. In real life, you're talking about individuals who leave prison with good intentions, but are met by a society that doesn't like criminals. Generally, they don't want to give them a chance, hire them, or feel optimistic about their future. We talk about programs to help these men and women find work, but they're few and far between, as are the employers who are willing to give them a chance and offer them decent wages. And, in some cases, parole conditions make it difficult for even low-level offenders to keep a job.

What happens as a result of all of these complications? Somebody who had every intention of turning over a new leaf goes back to growing marijuana, stealing, dealing drugs, or worse. And, let's not forget those men and women who are in jail, right now, for drug offenses that are no longer offenses at all. If that were you, how bitter would you be when you came out?

How jaded and frustrated would you be, and could you put on a good face, make a good impression, and work twice as hard as the average person just to barely make ends meet?

Those of us who are free must be the ones to give voice to this issue. Just as health care brings us back to that question of whether or not we are willing to care for the weakest among us, so does this issue. If we endeavor to be the land of the free, then we must answer the question of why we lead the world in incarceration of our citizens. We are caught in a fiscally reckless *war* that has actually made no reduction in drug access, yet has made our country less safe.

So, now we come back to the larger picture—to the state of our country as it stands, to our over-full prisons, our nonviolent criminals, and what comes next if we want our society to not just make ends meet, but go back to thriving as we once did. Remember, I told you it's all connected, and that's still the case.

Am I going to make the argument now that over-incarceration is the result of economic inequality or benefits economic inequality? Yes.

First, those who end up in prison are vastly, overwhelmingly, disproportionally representative of communities of poverty. The median annual income of those in prison, prior to incarceration, was $19,185 in 2014. That's less than 40 percent of the national average.[106] Their average was only *slightly* above the poverty line, in fact.[107] In short, those who struggle with poverty dramatically increase their likelihood of going to prison. (And, you should be connecting the dots now—more and more of our people are struggling with poverty every day.) Additionally, those who go to prison dramatically increase their likelihood of facing future poverty, and that future poverty generally ensures that they

---

106   Bernadette Rabuy and Daniel Kopf, "Prisons of Poverty: Uncovering the Pre-incarceration Incomes of the Imprisoned," Prison Policy Initiative, last modified July 9, 2015, https://www.prisonpolicy.org/reports/income.html.

107   Mark Gongloff, "45 Million Americans Still Stuck below Poverty Line: Census," *Huffington Post*, last modified November 8, 2017, https://www.huffingtonpost.com/2014/09/16/poverty-household-income_n_5828974.html.

go back to prison.[108] We're back to recidivism, and yet another primary cause of it. The cycle is rooted in economic struggles, and it should be obvious why. If you can afford food, you don't steal it. If you can't, you do.

Second, drug use is also tied directly to economic inequality. Our country is experiencing a heart wrenching opioid epidemic. This too is a symptom of economic inequality. Heroin addiction specifically is three times more likely in those who make less than $20,000 a year than those who make $50,000 or more. Research also indicates that a country with a healthy middle class and low or moderate levels of economic inequality sees lower addiction rates, with most kicking their addiction by age thirty.[109] To the contrary, as our inequality rises, since 2010, we've seen heroin deaths have quadrupled among men and women who are 25 to 34 years old.[110] Our opioid epidemic may, in fact, be one of our loudest reality checks that our middle class is disintegrating.

Is that the worst of the economic inequality surrounding our prison system? No. One word: *slavery.*

Not many Americans know that we have *millions* of people in unpaid, forced labor right at this moment. The Thirteenth Amendment abolished slavery for everyone except criminals, and we've created a system of justice to ensure we have more of those than any other country.

So who benefits from this slave labor? It's not shadow groups you've never heard of. It's Whole Foods. It's Victoria's Secret. It's Wal-Mart and McDonalds. AT&T, BP, Starbucks, Microsoft,

---

108   Sasha Abramsky, "Toxic Persons: New Research Shows Precisely How the Prison-to-Poverty Cycle Does Its Damage," *Slate Magazine,* last modified October 8, 2010, http://www.slate.com/articles/news_and_politics/jurisprudence/2010/10/toxic_persons.html.

109   Maia Szalavitz, "Addictions Are Harder to Kick When You're Poor. Here's Why," *The Guardian,* last modified June 1, 2016, https://www.theguardian.com/commentisfree/2016/jun/01/drug-addiction-income-inequality-impacts-recovery.

110   Alex Berezow, "Heroin Overdose Deaths Quadruple among Older Millennials," American Council on Science and Health, last modified January 5, 2017, https://www.acsh.org/news/2017/01/05/heroin-overdose-deaths-quadruple-among-older-millennials-10690.

Nintendo, American Airlines, and the lists goes on and on.[111] This is what helps the private prisons make profit. What exactly does this look like? In the example of Whole Foods, it meant sourcing cheese and fish produce farmed by inmates for as little as 74 cents per day. Starbucks utilized this labor for £10 per week (£.25 per hour) to prepare their bags of tea. In short, this population can and has been exploited at unfathomably low wages and without any worker's rights.

Is the point to call out these specific companies? *Absolutely not*. In some cases, these companies have had very plausible deniability when it comes to knowing where this work has been coming from. The Microsoft example, for instance, where products came through a subcontractor who was contracting work out to the prison system. Microsoft may or may not have known who was making their products. So, no, this isn't about calling out these specific companies; it's about showing you just how ubiquitous the use of prison workers is. This is such a core part of our economic engine that many of our most well-known companies are tapping into these mandatory, unpaid or essentially unpaid, avenues of slave labor, both knowingly and unknowingly.

Now, I need a minute to address one specific myth. Most people in this country already know that African Americans and Latino Americans disproportionately make up our prison population, so I want to clear something up here. As we have already established, higher levels of poverty lead to higher levels of incarceration, which both of these groups also grapple with. However, it's also true that we've all done something that could get us arrested, so why are these groups so disproportionately represented within our prison system?

There are people out there who believe there are reasons, other than economic desperation and the unfairness of our criminal justice system, which lead to the higher rates of incarceration that

---

111 Joanna Zambas, "10 Companies That Use Prison Labour to Rake In Profits," *Career Addict*, last modified October 11, 2017, https://www.careeraddict.com/prison-labour-companies.

we see in these communities. So, then we have to ask the question: Who commits the most nonviolent drug offenses? Well, the sort of person who *commits* the most nonviolent drug offenses and the sort of person who's *caught* committing the most nonviolent drug offenses differ vastly.

Caucasian kids are more likely to sell drugs, but African American kids are more than 3 times more likely to be arrested for the offenses. Said again, white kids are a larger portion of the population and are 45 percent more likely to sell drugs. Black kids are 3.6 times more likely to be arrested for selling drugs and 2.5 more likely to be arrested for possessing drugs.[112] This is not belief, or based on some tiny sample of our country's population. These are the statistical facts.

So, what does it all boil down to?

We aspire to be the land of the free, and we claim to be the land of the free, but we lead the world in incarceration in our prisons. Mostly due to a war on drugs, which has failed, given that access to drugs is only slightly more difficult than access to alcohol, and yet we spend billions of dollars a year on it.[113] It is possible this war on drugs has unintentionally actually done more to further poverty and inequality in our country than it has to actually reduce access to harmful drugs.

In this broken system, this cycle of imprisonment and re-imprisonment that punishes poverty, there is only one group that wins: the prison system. Private correctional facilities took in almost five billion dollars in 2014[114]—which is about $36,550 per prisoner per year, by the way.[115] The more we fill our prisons,

---

112   "How the War on Drugs Damages Black Social Mobility."

113   Benjamin Powell, "The Economics behind the U.S. Government's Unwinnable War on Drugs," The Library of Economics and Liberty, last modified July 1, 2013, http://www.econlib.org/library/Columns/y2013/Powelldrugs.html.

114   Martha C. White, "Locked-In Profits: The U.S. Prison Industry, by the Numbers," *NBC News,* last modified November 2, 2015, https://www.nbcnews.com/business/business-news/locked-in-profits-u-s-prison-industry-numbers-n455976.

115   "U.S. Prison Population Declined One Percent in 2014," Bureau of Justice Statistics, last modified September 17, 2015, https://www.bjs.gov/content/pub/press/p14pr.cfm.

the more resources we spend on our prison system as opposed to building infrastructure or making investments that grow the GDP. The rest of us lose, because the cycle of poverty to prisons, and prisons back to unemployment, poverty, and crime, hurts the entire economy, and it also hurts the lives of millions.

What do we do? It's an easy answer. Stop imprisoning nonviolent drug offenders and provide treatment to drug users. Each year, we've been spending billions on this drug war, and we see no results. This doesn't even account for the damage done on a human level nor the billions lost in economic potential from creating this poverty cycle.

If anything, we've seen ever increasing organized gangs and gang violence, because the demand for substances is going up and the industry operates outside our judicial system. It's time to end the war. Not to abandon those who need help, and not to avoid actually reducing the use of drugs. It's just time to admit the experimental *supply* side tactics have failed and we need to focus our resources on the *demand* side.

Other countries are already showing the way in successfully reducing demand. A 2012 review by researchers with the European Monitoring Centre for Drugs and Drug Addiction in reviewing the Swiss-style model have concluded "major reductions" in continued use of heroin; "major disengagement from criminal activities," and "marked improvement in social functioning" (e.g. stabling housing and higher employment).[116] In fact, they've also concluded that "[the Swiss-style model] saves money."[117] In short, the model to reduce demand, improve lives, reduce crime and simultaneously save tax payer money is right in front of us. And the Swiss aren't the only ones: Canada, Germany, Australia, and

116 "EMCDDA Report Presents Latest Evidence on Heroin-Assisted Treatment for Hard-to-Treat Opioid Users," European Monitoring Centre for Drugs and Drug Addiction, last modified April 19, 2012, http://www.emcdda.europa.eu/news/2012_en.

117 "EMCDDA Report Presents Latest Evidence on Heroin-Assisted Treatment for Hard-to-Treat Opioid Users.".

others are already following suit[118] and also showing results. We just have to follow the research and the examples of where success has occurred. We must then save our middle class economically, else we will only see more and more people fall to addiction as the research around opioids directly indicates.

Ending the war on drugs by eliminating mandatory minimums on nonviolent crimes would be the right step. Yet, we still must fix the economic problems that drive people to crimes both violent and nonviolent. That is how we reduce the human cost as well as the cost to economic growth. We need to stop investing in prisons and allowing for mass incarceration. Instead, let's invest in our communities to eliminate poverty. Let's invest that thirty billion a year we put specifically into the drug enforcement administration into specialized training and education for those who graduate without high school degrees. Let's teach entrepreneurship in common core classes, and help our citizens see, and believe in, choices.

Right now, there is no doubt that we have many individuals who ended up in prison primarily because they felt they were out of choices, and had no avenue to pursuing their own American Dream without turning to crime. We need to show our poverty-stricken communities that there is hope, and choice, before individuals, and especially their children, turn to crime. You would be hard pressed to find a mother and father who would watch their children starve before turning to crime. And, as men and women get out of prison, we need to do a better job of making sure that they also have choices.

Simply, we have to break the cycle of crime, unemployment and underemployment, and poverty. It hurts us to different degrees, but it hurts us all.

To that end, and perhaps most importantly, let's begin to research, test, and evaluate economic systems like Universal Basic Income, which could take a variety of forms. If we can

---

118 "Four Pillars Drug Strategy," City of Vancouver, accessed November 30, 2018, https://vancouver.ca/people-programs/four-pillars-drug-strategy.aspx.

reduce economic inequality, and eliminate poverty, we can in turn eliminate a supermajority of crime in our country. And, as I shared in earlier chapters, the research indicates we might even reduce our deficit and increase GDP in the process. That's a path the left and right could get behind, and one that could help us reclaim the mantle, "land of the free."

Chapter 7

Moral Leadership for the World

The fact that we've been discussing grand, treasured concepts such as the American Dream and whether we can still call ourselves the "land of opportunity" or "land of the free" should be a sign that our country is at something of a turning point. Whether you want to think of us standing on that precipice I spoke of earlier or not, the simple truth is that our current path is not sustainable. We have reached the peak of inequality in the last hundred years and, the last time this happened, our government pushed the New Deal. This time we're passing tax reforms that further shift the tax burden on those who are already struggling.

Since our nation began, we have struggled to do the right thing. At times, we have succeeded more than others, but we are losing some of the very principles that allowed us our strongest moments of leadership. On a local level, national level, and even a global level, we were willing to organize and speak truth about what mattered. Our citizens, all the way to our presidents, fought and died for ideas that transformed the world.

A moral leader is one whose authentic conviction allows them to withstand virtually unlimited pressure. They stand on immutable principles that ultimately put them on the right side of history. In the business world, they're referred to as authentic leaders. Often these people are hesitant to become leaders, because they are not driven by their ego, as most of their peers are. Yet, it is precisely this subtle difference that allows them to withstand the pressure that their peers would not. It allows them the conviction to do one of the most frightening things in human experience, let alone political leadership—be unpopular.

Talking about issues that poll well is far more popular than actually doing something about them. To take bold stances, whatever they are, will be unpopular to some. It's easy to win support for a vague promise. A specific plan will have critics. Yet, that is exactly *why* we have leaders in the first place. To see over the hill of popular opinion and take us somewhere better.

People have built great nations with a wide spectrum of opinions at play. However, great nations are not built by leaders who put their interests over their people, who deflect responsibility rather than take action, whose commitments can't be trusted, and who occupy their time with concerns of being popular.

We need leaders who show integrity with their commitments, take responsibility so that they can take action, and put service over self, again and again. These are the standards we all agree on, across the political spectrum. The loudest opinion, or the opinion of the wealthiest, need not win the day.

And here, you're probably going to see the last thing you thought you were going to see in this book. As someone who has run as a Democratic candidate for U.S. Congress, I will still give credit where it is due. President Trump will maintain his positions, no matter how unpopular they are, and in the face of all criticism. That is something that we should see in far more political leaders. (Notice, I am not saying he has always stuck to his positions, or that the positions themselves are right, but he doesn't change his positions due to political pressure from others, even members of his Cabinet or well-heeled special interest groups that got him elected.)

But there is one key distinction missing between this formula and the recipe we need, which I pray President Trump will begin to exhibit. Simply, you must stand against adversity when it comes to *ideas that are supported by your young citizens.* Why our youth? Because this is the direction your history will take. This is how you can stand on the right side of history. In this category, unfortunately, Trump is not taking positions supported by the generation to come, though I still hold out hope that he will—both for his own legacy and the legacy of our country, and for the people who need our government's help.

And besides that, if you build a wall that my generation will tear down, you're just wasting a lot of time and money. Let's be more fiscally conservative than that.

Banter aside, however, this really is what leaders like John F. Kennedy got right. During his time, Civil Rights was an incredibly unpopular and life-threatening political position to support, but an overwhelming majority of the upcoming generation supported it. Today, eight in ten Americans think it positively affected the country, and only 1 percent think it didn't.[119] But, in his time, members of his own generation were in large part against it. He listened to the youth, acknowledged what was right, and acted accordingly.

Kennedy, by the standards we now measure by, might be considered deeply flawed by some. Yet, I believe he gave his life for causes that meant something, inspired us to the stars, and made the decisions that saved the world from a nuclear holocaust. All in about half of one term as President.

The entire culture of our country emanates from the culture of our leadership, and if our leaders don't keep their personal word, then why would other countries trust that we will uphold our international agreements? If our leaders don't take personal responsibility for how they behave, and the people they represent, then how could other countries have confidence we will do our part in taking responsibility to solve the global crises of our time? The result of our failure in leadership will be that our people will suffer.

---

119 "Public Opinion on Civil Rights: Reflections on the Civil Rights Act of 1964," Roper Center for Public Opinion Research, accessed December 2, 2018, https://ropercenter.cornell.edu/public-opinion-on-civil-rights-reflections-on-the-civil-rights-act-of-1964/.

If we want leaders that lift us up again, especially in the era of social media, it's going to mean learning to love flaws and focusing on the values that matter. Not partisan, religious, or personal choice values. Such authentic, moral leaders are the only ones who can save us, however flawed they may end up being, but as Theodore Roosevelt once told us, those who dare greatly will also have great failures. If we want to find great leaders, we must, in fact, look beyond personal flaws and professional failings. Great leaders are born from adversity and have great compassion for they too are flawed:

> It's not the critic who counts; not the man who points out how the strong man stumbles, or where the doer of deeds could have done them better. The credit belongs to the man who is actually in the arena, whose face is marred by dust and sweat and blood; who strives valiantly; who errs, who comes short again and again, because there is no effort without error and shortcoming; but who does actually strive to do the deeds; who knows great enthusiasms, the great devotions; who spends himself in a worthy cause; who at the best knows in the end the triumph of high achievement, and who at the worst, if he fails, at least fails while daring greatly, so that his place shall never be with those cold and timid souls who neither know victory nor defeat.

Theodore Roosevelt, *Citizenship in a Republic*

At times, our country was seen by many as a moral leader for the rest of the world, and many of us were very proud of that. When Kennedy's temperance allowed us to avoid going quietly into the night of nuclear war in the Cuban missile crisis, we showed the character of our best self. When six days after 9/11, President Bush stood with American Islamic leaders to say we would not allow fear to drive our treatment of our fellow citizens, we showed how we could be the greatest country in the world.

We have taken care of ourselves, but we also worked on behalf of the global community when it came to what we believed in—

democracy, human rights, and, of course, freedom. Among the freedoms we fought for? The opportunity for every hardworking person to find prosperity.

Today, our world's greatest challenges all relate to that most basic of rights: survival. They include poverty, hunger, access to clean water, and the destruction of the world due to mankind's need for resources. Chief among all else, the destruction of our environment through pollution and global warming could kill more people than all prior wars combined. And although we absolutely must work to address the inequality and issues exhibited in our own United States, the question of protecting the environment must be solved both locally and globally.

In short, the most important moral issue of our time is how we save our planet. This is what will determine whether our country will once again be on the right side of history.

America must remain present in the crises of our world at large. This requires that we recognize the fact that our country is one voice in a global choir which needs to address, in whole, the future sustainability of our planet. Whether you believe in climate change or not, whether you feel that peak oil has already happened or not, or think that modification of our food is a concern or not, we are in this together. We have to lead, inspire, encourage, and support every nation in the world to work in collaboration and make sure our children have food, clean water, energy, and a safe planet to inherit. And, we cannot do that by withdrawing from the table.

Yet, the Paris Accord—also known as the Paris Agreement, the Paris Climate Accord, or the Paris Climate Agreement—is an agreement within the United Nations Framework Convention on Climate Change (UNFCCC) that deals with greenhouse gas emissions mitigation, adaptation, and finance starting in the year 2020. And the U.S., with the stroke of a pen under President Trump, is now the only country to reject the agreement.

That's right: we're the *only* country in the U.N. to reject it.

Brayden W.B. Olson

Faced with the most important moral, economic, and life-threatening crisis of our era, the United States has walked away.

For those who don't already understand the life-threatening implications of this decision, let me share more about the economic ones. When the United States chooses not to agree to reduce our carbon emissions, this action ultimately limits our ability to effectively compete in the growing green energy sector where most of the future job creation in the energy industry sector is coming from. It ties us to an *economic* sinking ship: fossil fuels. The rest of the world moves on and we stand still.

Our oil isn't going to last forever. The future will be covered in solar panels—and, no matter what side of the political spectrum you're on, that's a good thing. We just need to prepare for it. By acting now, we can subsidize and retrain every last worker for these easier, cleaner, safer, and better-paying future jobs.

We're all but removing ourselves from a global industry with real, moral consequences that will, without doubt, affect our standard of living as a society. By not working with the countries that are on the forefront of this initiative, we are at a huge disadvantage going forward in the energy producing sectors. We don't even save jobs today by being out of it. If we make the investments we need to make, however, we can make sure jobs are transitioned without being lost. But leaving the Paris Accord ensures that we will lose out on jobs, trade, and economic opportunity in the future.

We're essentially asking to be at a further disadvantage when it comes to economic growth, which will further the economic inequality that's already ripping the seams of our society, and only by electing moral, authentic, flawed leaders and taking a moral stand are we going to be able to address this issue and get back on the right track.

As we have already touched on, inequality is at the root of all the major issues we're discussing. Because an oligopoly of oil companies does not want us to move on with finding alternative ways of producing energy that will aid in our survival as a species, we're choosing to put a few short-term profits over our future existence.

Why in God's name would even the wealthiest people within our country want to pursue this course? After all, it doesn't even make long-term fiscal sense. It's only happening because only the poorest of our society will suffer first. The consequences aren't felt equally in our society. It's the poor that live near the dumps and the slums. It's the poor that starve first when food doesn't grow. The consequences won't be felt by these decision makers until their children or grandchildren come of age—when no human on the planet will be able to avoid the consequences.

Climate change is occurring on all continents and in the oceans, driving heat waves and other weather-related disasters. For the first time, the UN has designated climate change a threat to human security, because of the violent conflicts these shortages are fueling.

Yet, in the air-conditioned boardrooms a million miles away they will get bigger profits this quarter. Those profits will turn into campaign donations to the officials they control and the cycle repeats.

The rewards go to one party while the consequence is felt today by another. It's the old thought experiment. If you could push a button and receive $1,000,000, but someone you didn't know, somewhere in the world, would die, would you do it? This group of people at the top of our society, the ones who control these oil companies and those who vote on these issues in Congress, unfortunately proves that many would indeed push that button. It's the same decoupling of reward to one group of people with consequence dealt to another group of people that let to the housing and financial collapse of 2008.

The poorest people are the ones impacted the most by environmental change. It's not fair or right, but it's true. They are seeing the effects first, and they will also have the most difficulty speaking out about it and seeking change. Remember when we were talking about the people who are too busy struggling to survive, finding basic food and shelter, to spare thought for larger issues? You might be struggling, too, but if you're reading this book, you probably have at least a few spare moments to understand the state of things, and understand that we who can do so must find our voices before it's too late. We have to get our heads wrapped around this issue, and we have to deal with it going forward. And, remember: wealth gets more aggregated when a society's middle class is being decimated, pushing more and more people who are in the middle toward the poverty zone; soon, those who have time to read this book and think about those who are living in poverty *will* be the ones dealing with poverty in their own lives. In other words, chances are, this issue is going to affect your family far sooner than it will affect the families of those who are making money off of the bad decisions being made to favor profits over our environment and a sustainable future.

Beyond the simple choices, like our commitment to reducing carbon emissions, we have far more difficult environmental challenges to tackle. For instance, we are pressured to produce more food and enable those in poverty-stricken areas access to clean water; the resources necessary to provide for those needs are diminishing rapidly. Whether you accept the reality of climate change or not, those are just the facts.

You may live in a part of our nation that is itself seeing the effects of our world's environmental decline, through clean water shortages, more extreme weather causing forest fires, more frequent and powerful hurricanes, or even work shortages that are themselves a result of declining natural resources. Globally, we are already seeing food shortages due to climate change, but more than half of the world's population will feel this shortage by the end of this century.[120] This is a global issue, but it is also affecting our own neighborhoods and cities. It can't be ignored any longer, but the truth is that we're not just talking about the

---

120   Larry West, "Global Warming to Cause Food Shortages," ThoughtCo, last modified January 11, 2018, https://www.thoughtco.com/global-warning-to-cause-food-shortages-1203847.

environment here. We're talking about a lack of leadership to face difficult problems.

There is a strong conflict between protecting our environment versus producing the most crops, food, and water that our budgets can allow. The debate is on where to draw the line—how *much* environmental damage can our world sustain if it is for the purpose of supplying more crops, food, and water, producing just as much as our budgets will allow? This is what the left and the right side of politics is all about—deciding how this can best be accomplished.

However, on some level, the choice is another false either-or scenario. We're presented with the fact that populations all over the world, and even within our own country, are facing shortages of water and food, but ignoring the fact that food and water are wasted at an incredible rate in our society, as well as in many others. We're choosing the environment or production in a way that suggests we cannot protect our environment while also feeding the hungry and taking care of basic needs. Moral leadership would push us to make this distinction, looking at overall sustainability and *the right thing*…but we as a society are more focused on making money and scoring political sound bites.

When we think about all of these issues, and consider how they're playing out around the world, it seems apparent that the country that will lead the world in moral leadership must be leading the effort to protect the physical world itself. In decades past, our nation would have been the one to step forward and say, without any hesitation, *This is a difficult problem, but we're going to figure it out. We'll lead the way, and work together with every nation that's willing, to make a sustainable future which will not leave whole segments of our global society without a place to call home.* If you know anything of history, or if you're old enough to remember backward decades into the mid-twentieth century, you'll have no doubt that our country would have joined in solving this problem, like in the postwar years when the United States led a global agricultural revolution that saw farm production skyrocket, while also supporting the Marshall Plan that helped rebuild Europe. We did both. We would have been first up to volunteer in every way, shape, and form. Our country would have naturally stepped into the role of leadership—moral leadership—and our own elected leaders would have been at the forefront of the efforts.

Today, we just try to score political points debating the issue for our various lobbied-interests and handing out hot dogs when disasters strike. We've somehow become the caricature of political leadership rather than the real thing. Like actors playing the parts, we recuse ourselves from the actual climate change work and conversations, but show up when disasters strike for photo opportunities, a smile, and delivering some timely quotes.

Now, you're asking yourself the same question so many of us face when we watch the news every day: whatever happened to the time when we all looked up to our leadership here in America, and knew that people around the world envied the kind of leaders we had? When we trusted our leaders to do the right, moral thing, both here at home and abroad on a world stage?

Somewhere along the way we began to shrink. I think many would say since the Assassination of John and Robert Kennedy this change began from bold leaders to safe caricatures. Because of that, we are all paying the price.

And, I want to speak to the fiscally conservative minded out there about that price.

You may be reading this and thinking, *Who cares if our leadership is moral? The role of government is to build stability, maintain peace, and provide a strong economy.* And, yes, all that's true. But, leaving beside the fact that moral leaders will by default help with that *maintain the peace* part, moral leadership is good for business. In fact, it's so good for business that executives who are prime examples of authentic leadership find themselves atop the highest-performing companies in our country; anyone who studies the profession of business leadership will tell you this, and these leaders double the profits on average of the companies they run.[121] Are there exceptions? Sure there are, but in most cases, those rare companies are virtual monopolies that thrive in spite of their leader, rather than *due* to their leader. In this way, at least, a country is similar to a business, and moral leadership on either a national or global stage is what generally allows for a thriving, admirable community that has a sustainable future.

Considering the current climate of things (pun intended), you might be wondering how all this discussion of moral leadership relates to politicians, who are generally our most visible leaders. On one hand, I'm telling you a moral leader takes unpopular stances on principle, and on the other hand, in our society, politicians are elected—they have to seek a particular station and look for support among our people if they're going to end up representing our people in Washington. But what if I were to tell you that the best politicians among us are the people who, if they had their way, would just as soon not be politicians?

That is the hallmark of an authentic leader, which we have far too few of in the Capital.

The men and women who are the best leaders among us, the most suited to provide moral leadership in Washington, are more than willing to follow another path. In fact, today they do because of the nature of politics. They may have turned to business, community activism, or even academics. It's these humble leaders, who will only be attracted to politics once it becomes a place to really serve again, that we most need in these positions of authority.

These are the types of people who we need in Washington—conscientious, careful, moral leaders who are willing to sacrifice their time and energy for the greater good. They step forward because they must, and through great reservation, to provide a kind of leadership that is absent. As much as they've sacrificed to get there, and those sacrifices are considerable, an authentic leader

---

121   Jack Zenger, "Great Leaders Can Double Profits, Research Shows," *Forbes,* last modified January 15, 2015, https://www.forbes.com/sites/jackzenger/2015/01/15/great-leaders-can-double-profits-research-shows/#26844ccf6ca6.

would have to operate as if this were their last term, even on their first term. It's the only way. It's also why I believe so strongly in the value of term limits.

Any genuinely moral leadership involves the frontrunner displaying a wide range of skills and abilities. Egos are not predominant, and yet such a leader knows how to act with servitude, charisma, dignity, and with a large dose of righteous integrity. By their very nature, they persuade others to change for the better, and due to their understanding of humanity and social interaction, they are able to bring others to overcome obstacles, guiding change and progress with enthusiasm. With their vision, they help to diminish individualism and to foster a consensus outlook in order to bring a group of individuals together in a spirit of unity. They fight day and night to help angry, disparate groups understand what they have in common.

You'll see examples of this if you look to our history, in an era where great men like Martin Luther King and John F. Kennedy died in service, and to changes in society that were made for the greater good. You'll see it displayed by politicians, businessmen, activists, athletes, and even our students. You'll see examples from all corners of our society, where individuals have stepped forward and taken a stand because they felt compelled to do so on behalf of their communities or our society as a whole. The only place you see less and less of them today is in public office.

And when you see these examples, you'll also see proof that moral leaders are the conscience of their group and help to bind it together through both good times and bad. That's what we need now. Moral leaders who can be a conscience, and work for the greater good in a way that builds unity among all segments of society and spectrum.

Until there is a generation in this country where there are no longer men and women willing to die for causes they feel are right, we are still the United States of America. Yes, it's true that the people who are willing to stand up for their causes and beliefs are hard to find in the general population, but we have more than enough to fill our Congress and our state legislatures. It is just as hard to find leaders with the level of self-interest that currently flood our political offices, but our system has found them with ease. We just have a system today that is perfectly set up for finding these rare people who exhibit self-interest above all else— they're not the only ones who get elected to office, but they are, clearly, the vast majority.

Are you willing to spend 80 percent of your life calling people to ask for money so that you can wield power? Well, you're in luck, because today's system was made for you—and having seen the other side of this wall in my own Congressional run, I can speak from experience: it's nothing like I would have ever imagined from the outside.

With some small, albeit difficult, changes—like term limits and campaign finance reform—we could have a system that attracts authentic, moral leaders and sets them up for success. People who couldn't fathom spending 80 percent of their time raising money when there's suffering in the world that they could be doing something about.

In the final chapter, I'll talk about the solution to our system of government, but suffice it to say that it is possible.

It's true that America has not always provided moral leadership in the world, and we're not doing so particularly well right now. Yet, at times, we *have* earned this title, and truly served as a moral compass for global society. We have said, "You can kill me, but you cannot silence what I believe in." We have said, "Come here to escape terror. Help us build our vision of the world." We have said, "No, we will not plunge the world into darkness today. We will not escalate this crisis." And, by God, we have said, "We choose to do these and the other things not because they are easy, but because they are hard and because they are right."

Part of our loss of moral leadership is fact. Another part is perception. In the next chapter, we'll further explore the root of this change in perception.

Chapter 8

An Informed Populace

In today's world, political leaders are not our moral leaders: neither, for the most part, are corporate leaders, religious leaders, teachers, media personnel, or sports heroes. This is all new—in the past, all of these institutions provided a wealth of leadership and good role models.

What happened?

At some point after the mid-twentieth century, media began to realize that negative news was big business. After the Kennedy era, the Nixon Watergate scandal proved that some politicians really were crooks. We began to change what we wanted to read about or the media began to change what they wanted to write about. Either way, I grew up in an age where the assumption was every leader, political or otherwise, was either a crook or a not-yet-discovered crook. This isn't to say there is not a lot of abuse of power at the top, but today it's all that ever is discussed.

It is for this very reason that few in this country believe our political leaders to be anything other than self-interested. It's become colloquial in our society to assume everything that comes out of a politician's mouth is a lie. In fact, they occupy the lowest possible position in terms of our expectations of their moral values. We generally believe them to be selfish profiteers, out for fame or fortune, or both.

Twilight of the Idols

In my own experience, I saw this transition as well. Prior to becoming a candidate, I had worked on a variety of issues for years and held strong opinions about them that were accepted by all as genuine—until I became a candidate. It was as if a switch had been flipped, and then suddenly I couldn't possibly be doing or saying any of the things I was doing and saying for reasons other than my election. People have just been disappointed and lied to one too many times.

A headline about a scandal brings the crowd, but exonerations are a footnote at best.

No facet of any public or private profession has been left untouched by earth-shattering headlines, and Americans have lost trust in one profession after another.

You name it—the Boy Scouts, youth service bureaus, teachers, schools, churches, athletes, celebrities, and local shop owners… they all came under severe scrutiny for the immoral actions of some individuals within their ranks.

Now, I'm not saying that some of these individuals didn't deserve attention to their various transgressions. Many of them did, and I in no way mean to suggest that their victims should have been ignored or that they should have gone without notice. However, the media's moves toward focusing only on the negative, and seeking out the aberrations among largely moral groups, partly adds to further skepticism, doubt, and even outright disgust for whole segments of the population. Are there politicians, teachers, members of church leadership, celebrities, and athletes who are actively trying to serve as moral leaders and voices within our society? Yes, and there always have been.

The simple truth is that, because of the media's attention to negativity and scandal, to ratings and violence above anything else, you could name dozens of scandals from the last twelve months, but would struggle to name more than a handful of positive things done by our leaders over the last twelve years.

The only thing more popular than a negative story is a story with no substance at all. In the era of "click-bait" articles (articles published with little to no content value, with an intentionally engaging headline to get people to click on it), I would wager there are ten *substanceless* articles to every negative one, and ten negative stories to every positive one. Yet, there are vastly more actions of good than evil in our society.

It may not feel like it anymore, but if there really are more acts of good in the world each day, then how did we get to this place where all we hear about is one horrible leader after another?

The answer? There's just not enough profit in celebrating the good.

Seeking higher ratings, greater circulation, and more profit, media conglomerates can hardly wait to find improper behavior in every facet of society, and then demand maximum retribution. Americans are swayed by one scandal after another. We have become the country of scandalous impropriety, and countries across the globe have good reason to mock our hypocritical ideology. After all, how can we espouse being a moral leader in the world when seemingly every area of our own government, corporate affairs, social institutions, and judicial systems are being rocked by immoral activity?

Of course, every story of American hypocrisy sells well in other countries, so those are printed and consumed with fervor as well.

There are just as many honorable men and women in the ranks of these organizations, and in fact there are more of them than not, but writing and airing stories about those kinds of people doesn't sell nearly as many ads. And the negative attention, over the years, has had an effect.

We lost trust in our leaders, in the ability of anyone to very simply do the right thing, and now our go-to attitude is skepticism rather than hope. A generation or two ago, parents weren't afraid to have their children play outside or to walk to school. And a few bumps, bruises, and scars were seen to build character.

So, where did we go wrong? What the heck happened?

Twilight of the Idols

The rise of 24/7 news networks, beginning with CNN in 1980, and the movement to news networks being for-profit rather than acting as a public service that they were required to perform in order to maintain their media licenses, changed so much more than we realized. Television news coverage was transformed into a competitive industry focused on making profits. A public service that enriched everyone's lives and kept informed all parts of our population from the richest to the poorest became something much cheaper and less revered.

For those who can't remember, news used to be provided as a free public service in exchange for a media license. The three major broadcasting networks were free to generate as much revenue as they could with all the rest of their programming, but for that privilege we baked integrity into the system. Today, in the era when information couldn't be more accessible, it has become harder than ever to find sources that place integrity above clicks.

With this change, the mission of informing the populace, the cornerstone of our democracy, has been replaced with the mission of an extra couple of clicks. Not because of the many talented journalists who serve in these jobs, but because the game has changed around them. The job changed from being focused on informing our citizens about news to generating revenue. The definition of news changed because media outlets began demanding that news generate profits.

There was a time when news was not seen as entertainment. It was seen as a public service, and a necessary part of being a segment of the media; in fact, the American public actually considered some of its greatest journalists like Homer Bigart and Walter Cronkite to be moral leaders who reported on what mattered, when it mattered. News wasn't expected to generate profits. It was expected to defend democracy by providing unbiased, up-to-the-minute news on a local and global scale.

But, fear, stress, violence, and conflict draw in more ad revenue. Everyone turns their head to watch a train wreck. It's not a more accurate reflection of our world; it's just a more profitable one. It's also a reflection that has a decidedly negative focus, and whether or not you fault the media conglomerates for competing for viewers and profits in a way that prioritizes profits over reporting, the simple fact of the matter is that the focus on scandal and negative actions has had an impact on the way we see both our communities and our leaders.

Our leaders were *never* perfect, but you can tell two sides of every story. One side challenges every person in our society to be the better version of themselves. The other side leaves us in fear, and generates more money. We need to be covering the great things our leaders are doing. Does this mean we shouldn't cover scandals and horrible news? Absolutely, we should—we have to cover it. That attention is at the heart of what's the true power of an informed public. To be able to hold our government, and its leaders, accountable when it really matters. To create change when the people need an organized voice.

Yet, we've cried wolf so often now that the American people have become numb. If we needed to take action, it would be harder than ever to present an organized voice. In fact, many of us have gotten so overwhelmed we've simply tuned out the news, social media, and even politically charged conversations with our friends entirely.

But, if the incentives were to inform a public of what matters, we'd see a very different version of our nightly news.

It's hard to even know what's a scandal anymore, when 2 a.m. offensive tweets compete with the very real question of whether foreign governments are directly subverting our democratic progress, and it all gets the same amount of airtime. Is a celebrity's divorce worth more airtime than a vote in the Senate? Well, that's what generates the most cash, and that's what can be reported on in a fast, blaring headline. Is a sex scandal really worth more airtime than a true statesman who stood against all pressure to vote against their party on an issue of importance to the people of their district? Not in my view.

Twilight of the Idols

Bit by bit, the focus only on what generates a click takes away from each and every one of us. It sets up a generation to be so overwhelmed with worthless news that they are unable to stay informed on what does matter. As Thomas Jefferson said, "wherever the people are well informed they can be trusted with their own government."[122] In short, a democracy can only thrive when its people are well informed. Yet, with each passing day we become less informed about virtually everything that matters in all the noise about things that don't.

Again, we have to expect more from media, and we have to go back to having news that isn't expected to generate massive revenue, or even any revenue at all. After all, you don't have to look too closely to see the agendas of mainstream media, which are unabashedly prominent to anyone who cares to notice them. We should go back to requiring the major broadcasting stations to perform the news as a public service one hour a night, with no revenue.

America has taken the opposite stance of most other leading countries in terms of the news and media connection—American people are not informed, are led astray by the political agendas of those reporting the news, and they often don't know the truth of a story or understand any of its complexity. So there is no way they are going to hold their leaders accountable, as we currently have the tendency to blame one side or the other, rather than looking closely at the reality of any issues at all. It's why many of us feel we "live in different worlds" from those on the other side of the aisle. Each of us receives a biased perspective from whatever media we're watching, and none of us are really receiving the news as it once was defined.

Remember the purpose of news: it's meant to give us an understanding of the world beyond our own doorstep, and provide us a connection to our leadership, our representatives

---

122 "Thomas Jefferson to Richard Price," Library of Congress, accessed December 2, 2018, https://www.loc.gov/exhibits/jefferson/60.html.

who act on our behalf. In some ways, it's expected to lead us to understanding, if not to action.

Right now, only 17 percent of Americans have faith in their leadership, which is a lower percentage than ever before.[123] Every leader gets dragged through the mud for something. And with the media often promoting agendas or stories for the sake of business and profits, as opposed to truth alone, and constantly attacking the other side, there is no balance—no organizational wide integrity coming from any of our major news organizations.

Partisanship is a distraction, but it grabs attention. We no longer believe the two parties will ever agree on anything. Nowadays, people see right through to the business agendas of each major party and have no faith that leaders are looking to make anyone's life better but the business interests supporting them.

We've accepted, as an uncontested reality, that our leaders in Washington and in our state capitals work for other people. Not us. They work for the people who support them via paid speaking engagements, airtime, and independent expenditures. Not the people who elected them. If our interests and related concerns don't align with theirs, then our interests will be forgotten.

Reform is only impossible if you believe it is, because our country was founded with the very specific intention of making sure the government could always be reformed by the people, for the people. But, in order to seek reform, in order to seek change, we have to understand what's happening. You're reading this book because you instinctively know that you haven't been getting the big picture, but we need to be able to stay updated on issues, and the actions of our leadership, as well, and on a daily basis. That can only happen through news, so this isn't something we can dismiss as being a matter of media or entertainment; this discussion, and accurate news, is integral to our future.

---

123 "Public Trust in Government: 1958–2017," Pew Research Center, last modified December 14, 2017, http://www.people-press.org/2017/12/14/public-trust-in-government-1958-2017/.

Twilight of the Idols

And we have to again emphasize that none of this is the reporters' faults, or even the fault of the producers and news directors at your local television station, who answer to their corporate executives where people are making the real money. The reporters and journalists are doing what they are told to do in order to keep their jobs. It is the organizations themselves that have changed. The ethics of the corporate interests running the media have forced their agendas onto journalists. Institutions mold individuals to report in the manner of the agendas they wish to advance, and journalists who start out hoping to make a difference soon find that their careers are on the line if they don't learn to bend.

This was not the case fifty years ago, or even thirty years ago, when many journalists were able to serve the people by keeping us truly informed about the things that mattered.

You aren't crazy when you think that mainstream media is biased; at the very least, media corporations are prioritizing profits and sound bites over full and accurate news; you are seeing what millions of other Americans are seeing, too, and they are equally as baffled by the turn of events. Even our late-night comedians and talk show hosts are supplied with politically biased agendas in alignment with their particular network, and yet, ironically, more and more Americans are turning to these comedians for their news. John Oliver, with the in-depth if not comical research and background they provide on every story, is one great example. While comedy, it provides more detail, research, and background than any of the other modern news programs I am familiar with.

Where is the well-rounded news on the issues that matter, though? How many Americans, quite literally, turn to the BBC and international news outlets to try and inform themselves about our own country? I know dozens, personally.

Most of us know what our President tweeted this week and who got offended by it, but how many Americans know that, right now, we only have half the rate of homeownership among our Millennial generation than China has? Remember that homeownership in our upcoming generation has also hit a record low for our nation. Our middle class is disappearing and, at best, we're discussing the latest tweet we disagree about; at worst, we're actually seeing and digesting fake news about how well the economy and Millennial homeownership are going.

As our world view darkens, so also follows our TV, movies, games, and media. From the late '30s through the early '80s, our heroes in books, games, television, and movies generally led by moral example. As we have lost faith in our leaders, the heroes in our media have also changed. As one commenter put it, "(Our heroes became) reflective of an era no longer imbued in optimism."[124] Today, many of our most popular shows feature main characters, or more than one, who has some serious disorder, ranging from antisocial personality disorder to narcissistic personality disorder on to just plain being a murderer.

This wasn't the case a few decades ago, but it now reflects the skepticism in our society, and what we expect to see. It's a consequence of every story we see pointing out once again that there are no good leaders left.

One of the biggest ironies is that the kind of leaders we need—authentic, moral leaders—are inspiring *and* flawed. They're flawed because they share their flaws, rather than hiding them from view. They're vulnerable on purpose. It's their humanity that they are sharing. After all, our leaders are exactly the same kind of humans we all are. The choice is simply whether they share their humanity openly or hide it from view.

In an era where media profits from scandal, we only allow those with perfect exteriors to become leaders. Unfortunately, these are most often the kinds of leaders who spend considerable time putting skeletons in closets.

In the study of authentic leadership, business leader and bestselling author Bill George describes these archetypes as

---

124 David Koepsell, "The Twilight of the Superhero," *International Policy Digest,* last modified August 29, 2015, https://intpolicydigest.org/2015/08/29/the-twilight-of-the-superhero/.

Twilight of the Idols

Rationalizers or *Glory Seekers*. A Rationalizer appears to be perfect because they deny and project all of their failings or shortcomings onto others. They shift blame, and they make it stick anywhere but to their suit jackets. A Glory Seeker appears to be perfect because their thirst for acclaim is unquenchable. They're more concerned with appearing on lists of the most powerful people than using their power for literally any productive purpose.

So, therein lies the challenge. In the era of social media, and everything being on camera, we've got a choice. We either elect leaders who appear perfect and slowly destroy our country, or we learn to love flawed leaders who really do work in the best interests of the people.

If our news media won't change, then we as a people have to.

If we want our news to change, then it is time for us to remove the profit motive and get back to journalism. For us to enlist their help in providing the checks and balances that an objective source of news provides, so that our people can be truly informed, on a day-to-day basis, about what matters. We need to get back to a system where media companies are required to provide the news as a public service, at least one hour per night, and it should be commercial-free so that they can't make money on advertising or worry about the profit margin during that hour. Does that mean shutting down the blogs and websites? No. Does it mean telling CNN to pack up? Again, no. But, if major media companies are required to provide this service of offering news as a public good, I think the demand of the American people for more objective news will quickly follow. The blogs, websites, and current news networks can adapt, join, or not.

We need a trusted source of media that we can, on a daily basis, depend on for morally objective, non-political news. What matters, as opposed to what makes money or what's popular to say.

But I'm part of this, and you're also part of this. We can't keep casting blame on others. It may not be your fault when someone rear-ends your car, but it is your responsibility how you decide to react to it. This is the system we have allowed to flourish around us, and there's nobody to blame but ourselves. And this sense of responsibility, of ownership, by the way, is the hallmark of an authentic leader—to take responsibility for their lives, their actions, and for their ability to help those around them.

In this case, we must do the same thing. Embrace flaws, stop clicking on outrageous stories, and support subscription journalism from outlets we trust. It's not our fault that we are here, but it is our responsibility to decide where we go from here.

Great people make mistakes. Sometimes great countries do, too. However, it is precisely this failure—and the challenges, struggles, and setbacks that come along with it—that build our character. If we can re-claim moral leadership, the lessons we have learned in this past era will make us stronger than ever.

Chapter 9

Give Me Your Huddled Masses

Our country has a long, prosperous, and fruitful history of immigration. We were even built by immigrants. And while immigration is a politically charged issue today, no one denies it has been a key part of our history. In fact, it has been so central to our principles and development that our openness to immigrants long ago became one of our fundamental, globally recognized values.

You may or may not know that the Statue of Liberty was a joint project between the United States and France, whereby they delivered the statue and we built the pedestal. What is especially little known now is that the funds were raised by ordinary citizens. On both sides. In France, even school children contributed to this foreign monument. In the United States, one of the "American Committee" members was nineteen-year-young Theodore Roosevelt, who helped raise money for the project. When we were gifted the Statue of Liberty, it was meant to represent the contributions our nation had made to the world at large—in being a beacon of freedom to those who shared our ideals around the world. At the bottom was famously inscribed a poem by Emma Lazarus, which itself raised money for the statue; it ends:

Brayden W.B. Olson

Give me your tired, your poor,
Your huddled masses yearning to breathe free,
The wretched refuse of your teeming shore.
Send these, the homeless, tempest-tost to me,
I lift my lamp beside the golden door!

This poem became the very basis on which funds were raised by an idealistic Roosevelt and the American Committee. Yet, today, we live in a very different country, in a very different time, and under very different circumstances. And we cannot agree on where our nation stands when it comes to welcoming immigrants, or simply sending them away to wherever else they can find a home.

In these divisive times, the left tends to unfairly characterize the right's position as, *They want to kick vulnerable children out of our country because they are racists.* In fact, that is no rational person's opinion. In the same way, the right misrepresents the left's position as, *They want to take in everyone, even terrorists, and allow any immigrant who wants to live off of welfare.* Again, a position that isn't held by any rational adult.

The positioning of each view, yet again, is divisive, but fear of our country continuing to celebrate and welcome immigration tends to tie back to economic inequality. For some people within our country, there's enough fear over the future that one of our fundamental principles is worth reconsidering, and so immigration is attacked. The right's position against immigration is more aptly stated: *New immigrants are a burden on our country because they take our jobs, housing, and other resources we are struggling to survive on.* In other words, summed up, people have turned against immigration because they feel that our own citizens aren't making it—we need help, and we can't afford to share opportunity that we don't have. Basically, we're afraid that our population can't support further immigrants. Not because we haven't benefited from them, but because it is easier to forget how much we've benefitted and been built by them than it is to accept that larger and more systematic change is what we need. Yes, we have a lot of people in need—I'm with you on that. But deporting immigrants or halting immigration isn't going to make the situation any better.

I'll explain what's really happening, and how we can really solve this problem, but I want to stop here and call out the factual issue that is causing this breakdown in communication.

In framing the immigration debate, liberals tend to focus on the needs of refugees and low-income earners, who are the most vulnerable immigrants and have the least ability to make their way through our byzantine immigration system. The left constantly talks about immigrants as being a group of day laborers and low income earners who need to be protected. Is this partially true? Yes, because every population has people who fit into this category, and yes, countries are measured by how they treat their most vulnerable.

This point is, however, the completely wrong point for us to be making when we talk about immigration. We don't lose jobs to immigrants. We simply don't. They have historically and continue today to create massive wealth and new jobs in this country.

Elon Musk, founder of Tesla and Spacex, is an immigrant. Sergey Brin, founder of Google, is an immigrant. Jeff Bezos' stepfather an immigrant. Steve Jobs' father, an immigrant. I can't imagine how much worse off we would be without Apple, Google, Tesla, Amazon, eBay, and Yahoo,[125] but also, if we look to our history, without Einstein, Nikola Tesla (the inventor), and Alexander Graham Bell (you know, telephones?). I know, I know, I get it—it's easy to point to outliers, so I'll point out this, as well. The U.S. benefits from more immigrant inventors than any other country in the world. By almost *ten times over* the next closest country.[126] That's how many patents are filed by immigrants who

---

125 Jeff J. Roberts, "7 Well-Known Tech Firms Founded by Immigrants or Their Children," *Fortune,* last modified January 30, 2017, http://fortune.com/2017/01/30/tech-immigrant-founders/.

126 Dan Kopf, "The US Has More Immigrant Inventors Than Every Other Country Combined," *Quartz,* last modified January 24, 2017, https://qz.com/890943/the-us-has-more-immigrant-inventors-than-every-other-country-combined/.

move into our country, which is almost two hundred thousand patents over the ten years tracked. In other words, some of the best and the brightest individuals around the world choose to come to the U.S. and share the benefit of their talents, their intelligence, and their success with our nation, people, and economy, above all others.

Now, you're used to the argument against immigrants pointing out people who come here penniless, without anything more than the clothes on their backs and their own wits to support them. Perhaps they even come by raft, hoping to reach our shores and find refuge. But I want to ask you: Why is that a bad thing?

These are men and women, and in some cases children, who struggled mightily to reach our shores. They were brave enough and smart enough to survive doing so, and they have the courage to believe in the American Dream, in the opportunity that can be found here, and that they are better off—that their families will be better off—if they become a part of this nation. They are, in general, more than willing to work hard, and to work for every penny and meal they'll get, if we'll only allow them to try their hands at seeking the opportunity that so many before them have sought out.

These are not the men and women who will keep your twenty-two-year-old college graduate sleeping in his old bedroom because he can't afford his own apartment or find a job in the downtown business district. They are, perhaps, a scapegoat for our problems, if we allow them to serve as such, but they are absolutely not the cause of the systemic decline that we're seeing across our society—not by any stretch of the imagination.

In short, the real message we need to discuss is why in the heck we should start turning away immigrants now. After all, we've had *incredible* return on investment. Our immigrants have been, and continue to be, some of our hardest working job creators in the country, and by God, we need to strengthen our economy. And they will help us if we allow them to do so, with their will, their work ethic, their intelligence, and their heart. While we do need to protect against those who would intend to do us harm, our economy would only benefit from a much more open border policy.

So, when we're turning away immigrants, or supporting anti-immigration legislation, what we're really supporting is a fear that we are not only in decline, but falling apart, and that the smallest thing—a single individual in need—could break us.

And therein lies the real problem. The people who don't want more immigrants to cross our borders have an absolutely valid concern. A concern every single American should be united behind.

Our economy is restructuring in a way I don't think we fully understand yet. Since the mid-1980s, the top .01 percent of earners, whose net worth exceeds $100M, saw their percentage of wealth nearly triple from 4 to 11 percent of our total economy by 2014.[127] This trend has only continued with the 1 percent's ownership increasing another 3 percent since 2013.[128] In the meantime, the households with less than $4M in wealth all saw a relative decline.

The concern all Americans should be uniting behind is this means our next generation isn't transitioning into a financially stable way of life. Whether this takes the guise of a lifetime of debt, the cost of living going up while wages stagnate, the inability to own homes, the growth of the gig economy, or more citizens falling into outright poverty, we have an economy headed to disaster in the area of automation. And we don't have significant economic paradigm reform in place to move us toward systems like UBI. Globalization has allowed low-skilled workers from around the world, whose cost of living is massively lower than here in the United States, to compete directly and eliminate jobs

---

127 Hargreaves, "Rich, Really Rich, and Ultra Rich."

128 Christopher Ingraham, "The Richest 1 Percent Now Owns More of the Country's Wealth Than at Any Time in the Past 50 Years," *The Washington Post,* last modified December 6, 2017, https://www.washingtonpost.com/news/wonk/wp/2017/12/06/the-richest-1-percent-now-owns-more-of-the-countrys-wealth-than-at-any-time-in-the-past-50-years/?utm_term=.9887fc21b26d.

across the country. No regulation or rollbacks are going to fix that. Even if we could, we shouldn't. These jobs are low-paying, and those that aren't already being done through automation will be shortly.

The problem isn't globalization or immigrants, though—it's an elimination of jobs with livable wages, and it's happening faster than our economic paradigm can respond to it.

You might say, *But look...we are near full employment, jobs are growing, and the stock market is doing fantastic.* To you, I have to respond, it's true that people are employed, but only because the economy has shifted toward gig jobs and underemployment. Employment isn't the problem. It's the distribution of wealth. We can be at full employment with a growing GDP and stock markets flying through the roof, but if during that time 99 percent of our households are becoming poorer and the majority of American children will be worse off than their parents were we, as a country, are failing economically and spiritually.

Think about this. For roughly every two people we've added to our population, we see one new person enter poverty. We can squabble about year-to-year changes, but that's about the picture we live in today.[129] [130] Imagine how that plays out over the course of a generation.

That's why many perceive immigrants with fear or anger. In a world where our children are struggling to survive—and in recent years almost half of our population growth is moving into poverty—any loss of any job in a community or family matters. Yet the immigrants didn't do this. The politicians who've been proudly proclaiming the economy has *bounced back* did.

Now, you fall into one of two categories:

---

129   "U.S. Population," Worldometers, accessed December 2, 2018, http://www.worldometers.info/world-population/us-population/.

130   Bob Bryan, "There Are 9 Million More People Living in Poverty Now Than before the Great Recession," Business Insider, last modified September 30, 2015, http://www.businessinsider.com/9-million-more-people-poverty-than-2007-2015-9.

Twilight of the Idols

In the first case, you understand everything I am saying, and you're with me, and this has already happened to you or someone in your family. You personally know people who are living in poverty, or on the edge of it, if you're not there yourself. As a result, you know why people are scared and angry and worried about losing their jobs when they're already underemployed. Heck, there's a good chance that you're scared about the very same thing, and about making ends meet. Maybe, even as you're reading this, you're afraid your boss is going to fire you and hire someone else because you called out sick with the flu for a week last month. Now, you're not only trying to pay the bills that didn't get paid because you were out sick, but you're terrified that time out of work is going to lose you your job entirely. You know where this country stands, but you don't necessarily know what to do about it.

If you're in the second category, you're doing all right, or maybe you're even doing very well right now. If you've got more than $1,000 in savings, you're already ahead of most Americans and in this category. Maybe you've been working overtime, six or seven days a week, just to make sure you stay ahead of the game and don't fall behind. Now that you've got some money in savings, you figure things are looking up, and maybe things aren't so bad as you thought. Or, perhaps you're really ahead of the curve—you're a doctor, lawyer, or in some highly specialized trade that only needs to worry about these issues as they impact others.

By no means do these economic positions define your stance on immigration, but this is all tied together.

Immigration won't break the economy. Our economic paradigm and political leadership will. No matter which of these categories you live in, AI will replace high-skilled workers just as fast as automation will replace low-skilled workers. Today, AI is already decreasing the amount of billable hours for lawyers, which is eliminating new positions.[131] It's happening right now.

---

131 Steve Lohr, "A.I. Is Doing Legal Work. But It Won't Replace Lawyers, Yet," *The New York Times,* last modified March 19, 2017, https://www.nytimes.com/2017/03/19/technology/lawyers-artificial-intelligence.html.

Across the board, skilled professions are poised to start seeing jobs disappear. All Americans, in both categories, face the same challenges and keeping immigrants out won't impact this outcome one bit.

And that is the real point. If you're concerned about immigration, you're probably *actually* concerned about the economic struggles experienced by you, your family, or your community—and that is very real. It's also about to become real for parts of our population where it wasn't before. The glass buildings and ivory towers of our cities will find this wave of new technology to be fundamentally different than new technology that created jobs in the past.

Perhaps this realization is why support for immigrants has been growing since the '90s, despite what some politicians would have you believe. In fact, in 1994, 63 percent of Americans said immigrants where a burden to our country, but by 2016, 57 percent said they are actually strengthening our country, as Millennials are far more likely to see immigrants as a welcomed force in the economy.[132] [133] That's a complete reversal of the majority viewpoint. The trend is also likely to continue moving in this direction; as those who see immigrants as a strength to the U.S. follow a generational trend, with growing support among the Silent, Boomer, Gen X, and Millennial generations at 41, 48, 60, and 76 percent, respectively.

Simply put, immigration isn't the problem. In large part, we don't even disagree about it. Like partisan politics, this red herring pulls us away from the issues that actually do need to be addressed in our country, our leadership, and our economy.

---

132   Bradley Jones, "Americans' Views of Immigrants Marked by Widening Partisan, Generational Divides," Pew Research Center, last modified April 15, 2016,   http://www.pewresearch.org/fact-tank/2016/04/15/americans-views-of-immigrants-marked-by-widening-partisan-generational-divides/.

133   "Campaign Exposes Fissures over Issues, Values and How Life Has Changed in the U.S.," Pew Research Center, last modified March 31, 2016, http://assets. pewresearch.org/wp-content/uploads/sites/5/2016/03/3-31-16-March-Political-release-1.pdf.

Twilight of the Idols

The issue of immigrants is a distraction from the real issue: more and more Americans are being left behind. By globalization, by automation, by AI, and by a tax code that is making it easier to live off of wealth without working and harder to earn a dollar through hard work.

Instead of talking about immigration, or trying to close our borders, we need every mind in this country focused on the real problem.

We should embrace immigration as part of a plan to *improve* our economy through job and wealth creation. We should also embrace it to reclaim this part of the American spirit, and a supermajority of our upcoming generation are already on board. Right now, very simply, we need every idea we can get about how to move forward and build a stronger economy, a more sustainable future, and a stronger middle class. The immigrants who've lived within our borders, and the immigrants hoping to come to our shores still, are not the enemy. They're being set up to be viewed as such, perhaps, but where you come down on that issue has nothing to do with the fact that our country was developed through freedom of culture and expression, and immigrants were integral to our getting where we are today. If immigrants of either today or yesterday, or any time past, are willing to stand up beside the rest of us and work for the solutions we need, and come together to fight economic inequality, then we should welcome their voices and understand that the precipice we're standing on has everything to do with the poverty that is threatening our middle class. If you're on the verge of falling over that cliff, it has far less to do with whether your family has been here for one generation or for ten, and a lot more to do with the economic and political consolidation we began in the 1980s.

One way or another, the largest challenge that lies before us isn't coming together on this issue, but it is integral that we not allow it to distract us, or serve as a scapegoat for the difficulties our country currently faces. We are where we are, today and we need real solutions and active steps forward. Arguing over who is the more authentic American citizen won't get us there.

Instead, we must take back our government in order to ensure a future where this next generation will have the same opportunity the last one did to get out of poverty, so that our country's citizens, wherever they came from originally, have a hope for not just a better future, but any future at all.

In our final chapters, we'll explore exactly how to do this.

Chapter 10

Glorious Future

We Americans are an optimistic people. We always have been. It's part of the ethos that has driven our country forward. It's why despite the fact that our current generation is headed toward becoming the first in American history to do worse than our parents, a full 53 percent still believe they can defy the odds and become millionaires.[134] This is not a flaw. It is our hope. It goes back to the American Dream that so many of us grew up hearing about. A dream that through hard work you could achieve wealth, freedom, and purpose while building a family and a moral life. A dream which has brought so many brave men and women to our country since it was founded.

But, we cannot govern only with our hope or we will lose this dream for this and future generations.

This dream, and this optimism, has been an asset that has helped build this country, foster independence, and overcome momentous challenges. Yet, we live in an era of dwindling idols. Optimism, in a world where hard work leads to poverty, is a broken promise.

---

134 Julia Glum, "53% of Millennials Expect to Become Millionaires One Day, according to a New Study," *Time Magazine*, last modified June 11, 2018, http://time.com/money/5308043/millennials-millionaires-new-research/.

Brayden W.B. Olson

We overcame our challenges in the past because our leaders supported a culture, a spirit of a people, who were ever resilient. Today, our leaders tap into this optimism to belittle the challenges we truly face. They tell us that the economy has bounced back, when 99 percent of us have slipped further downward.

As the wealth gap widens, we watch the twilight of the American Dream. This is the crisis of our modern era. The results of which will impact health care, the global climate, the stability of government, and virtually every other issue that we as a people care about.

31 percent of U.S. adults are struggling to get by[135], and 61 percent are one $1,000 medical bill or one missed paycheck away from financial collapse.[136] Since 2000, 4 percent of our middle class has disappeared and the income that defines the middle class has also shrunk.[137] [138]

As our own President shared with us in December of 2013, "It is harder today for a child born here in America to improve her station in life than it is for children in most of our wealthy allies, countries like Canada or Germany or France. They have greater mobility than we do."[139]

---

135 "Report on the Economic Well-Being of U.S. Households in 2015," Board of Governors of the Federal Reserve System, last modified May 2016, https://www.federalreserve.gov/2015-report-economic-well-being-us-households-201605.pdf.

136 Quentin Fottrell, "Millions of Americans Are One Pay Check Away from the Street," MarketWatch, last modified January 20, 2018, https://www.marketwatch.com/story/most-americans-are-one-medical-emergency-away-from-financial-disaster-2017-01-12.

137 Richard Fry and Rakesh Kochhar, "The Shrinking Middle Class in U.S. Metropolitan Areas: 6 Key Findings," Pew Research Center, last modified May 12, 2016, http://www.pewresearch.org/fact-tank/2016/05/12/us-middle-class-metros-takeaways/.

138 "The American Middle Class Loses Ground Nationally," Pew Research Center, last modified May 11, 2016, http://www.pewsocialtrends.org/2016/05/11/1-the-american-middle-class-loses-ground-nationally/.

139 "Remarks by the President on Economic Mobility," The White House: President Barack Obama, last modified December 4, 2013, https://obamawhitehouse.archives.gov/the-press-office/2013/12/04/remarks-president-economic-mobility.

Twilight of the Idols

With more effort than ever needed to sustain day-to-day living, many people have turned their focus to immediate survival as these critical pieces of our cultural identity slip away.

When we speak about the future, there is often one issue that takes particular focus: *What will life be like for our children, and the next generation?* This is our greatest challenge. And this is where Americans look at what is happening in our country and, with a broad, unified, bi-partisan voice answer. Only 6 percent of Americans feel that the world will be better for their children based on research by the American Council on Science and Health. Yet, seven times as many Chinese citizens feel optimistic for their own future generations, and the same can be said for almost three times as many citizens of Saudi Arabia.[140]

They're optimistic because their children are transitioning to middle-class lifestyles, building savings, and starting families. As discussed before, Millennials in China have double the rate of homeownership than we do. As their future strengthens, we experience the lowest rate of homeownership we've ever seen. As their incomes rise, 99 percent of us are in stagnation and decline, all while our country's debts mount ever higher.

Our future is defined by what happens and is happening to our youngest generation of workers.

It's true that we are seeing lower levels of Millennials in full employment when compared to any of the last three generations during this same age period,[141] that more of us are living at home than at any time in recorded U.S. history,[142] that we have over a

---

140   Alex Berezow, "Only 6% of Americans Think the World Is Getting Better," American Council on Science and Health, last modified July 3, 2016, https://www.acsh.org/news/2016/07/03/only-6-of-americans-think-world-is-getting-better.

141   Richard Fry, Ruth Igielnik, and Eileen Patten, "How Millennials Today Compare with Their Grandparents 50 Years Ago," Pew Research Center, last modified March 16, 2018, http://www.pewresearch.org/fact-tank/2018/03/16/how-millennials-compare-with-their-grandparents/.

142   Richard Fry, "It's Becoming More Common for Young Adults to Live at Home – and for Longer Stretches," Pew Research Center, last modified May 5, 2017, http://www.pewresearch.org/fact-tank/2017/05/05/its-becoming-more-common-for-young-adults-to-live-at-home-and-for-longer-stretches/.

trillion dollars in student debt on our shoulders alone,[143] and that we're the first generation in American history to be projected to be financially worse off than our parents.[144] These are the facts. It's not hopeless, but only radical change will help.

If you're not a Millennial, or an iGen, you might say, *Phew, not my problem.* And despite the fact that I'm a Millennial, I am likely one of the few that will be okay when others aren't. That doesn't change the fact that this is the most important challenge facing my personal life, because we thrive or die as a society. As an interconnected culture, country, and people.

I know this sounds like a generational issue, but it is the exact opposite. Our youngest working generation is always the canary in the coal mine when it comes to the strength of our economy. As the U.S. Chamber of Commerce Foundation said in a November 2012 study on the issue, "The young adult workforce is usually the last to be hired and first to be fired."[145] What is happening to everyone, and the fate ahead of all of us, generally affects them first.

And what does this mean for you, regardless of your generation or even the ages of your children? It means the air in that mine is getting thin quickly—for all of us. The suffering of *most* of our citizens cannot be ignored in a society that will have a strong future.

The future of our economy, especially when looked at beside the question of how Millennials fit into our workforce, is one of those rare issues where we're all so well-aligned that it's hard to find any conflicting opinions or research that the Millennial

---

143 April Lane, "Beyond the Headlines: Is Student Debt Strangling Millennials' Chances for Success?" Bentley University, accessed December 2, 2018, https://www.bentley.edu/impact/articles/beyond-headlines-student-debt-strangling-millennials-chances-success.

144 "The Fading American Dream," Opportunity Insights, accessed December 2, 2018, https://opportunityinsights.org/.

145 "The Millennial Generation Research Review," U.S. Chamber of Commerce Foundation, last modified November 12, 2012, https://www.uschamberfoundation.org/reports/millennial-generation-research-review.

generation is headed toward economic hardship and economic inequality is to blame. If there is an argument to be had, though, it tends to go along these lines: either the economy is doing better than ever because overall unemployment is low (even if more are struggling than ever), levels of employed Millennials are low because they're just staying in college longer, or Millennials are just lazy, lacking a work ethic (alternately, you can insert your favorite generational pejorative here). I'll tackle each.

The argument that the economy is doing well because unemployment is low fails to take into account many of the most critical factors we *should* be considering. For instance, how is unemployment being calculated…are people making enough at their full-time jobs to survive?

Since the '80s, the middle-class real wages have alternated between stagnation and decline.[146] Real costs for food, housing, and education are skyrocketing while income declines.[147] After-tax middle-class incomes in Canada are now much higher than in the United States. The poor in Europe earn more than the American poor.[148] Our middle class is losing ground every year.[149]

At the same time, we've *tripled* the GDP and wealth of our country.[150]

146 Drew DeSilver, "For Most U.S. Workers, Real Wages Have Barely Budged in Decades," Pew Research Center, last modified August 7, 2018, http://www.pewresearch.org/fact-tank/2018/08/07/for-most-us-workers-real-wages-have-barely-budged-for-decades/.

147 Jennifer Erickson ed., "The Middle-Class Squeeze," Center for American Progress, last modified September 24, 2014, https://www.americanprogress.org/issues/economy/reports/2014/09/24/96903/the-middle-class-squeeze/.

148 David Leonhardt and Kevin Quealy, "The American Middle Class Is No Longer the World's Richest," *The New York Times*, last modified April 22, 2014, https://www.nytimes.com/2014/04/23/upshot/the-american-middle-class-is-no-longer-the-worlds-richest.html.

149 "The American Middle Class Is Losing Ground," Pew Research Center, last modified December 9, 2015, http://www.pewsocialtrends.org/2015/12/09/the-american-middle-class-is-losing-ground/.

150 Kimberly Amadeo, "US GDP by Year Compared to Recessions and Events," The Balance, last modified October 23, 2018, https://www.thebalance.com/us-gdp-by-year-3305543.

How does that pencil out? Simply, our economy can grow substantially and everyone can be fully employed while simultaneously sending 99 percent of our population into decline. It's only a question of distribution.

Unemployment can be at historically low levels while jobs pay barely or below subsistence wages. We can force a generation into a "gig economy," working long hours where they make less than they need to pay their bills and exist without any long-term security on which to build families or communities.

We've also seen a historically unprecedented separation between rising productivity (output) and stagnating wages paid to the workers who made it happen.

Now, let's move to another frequently cited sign of a strong economy. When we say the economy is doing well because stocks are doing well, we fail to account for the fact that stock ownership is the lowest it's been in two decades.[151] Most Americans aren't participating, and the wealthiest 10 percent of Americans own almost ten times as much stock (the top 10 percent owns over 80 percent of all stocks in fact) as the 40 percent of Americans below them—who, it's important to note, are still above average when it comes to wealth.

In short, yes, the economy is strong for a small slice of the country and grows stronger every year. If you're one of those in a position where you're already doing well, then *your* economy has indeed recovered. Yet, every year our economy becomes more fragile and ever closer to a collapse that will impact the wealthiest among us. For the wealthiest who are truly not impacted by these trends for now, you might genuinely think this matter is being blown out of proportion.

Most Americans, however, aren't experiencing this same economy.

With questions of employment and underemployment in mind, we can turn to the next point. How about all those

---

151 Robert Frank, "The Stock Gap: American Stock Holdings at 18-Year Low," *CNBC*, last modified September 4, 2014, https://www.cnbc.com/2014/09/08/the-stock-gap-american-stock-holdings-at-18-year-low.html.

Millennials who just love going to college? The same U.S. Chamber of Commerce Foundation report from 2012 also answered this objection for us. "In down markets, when jobs are harder to find, many Millennials make the choice to stay in school, lowering the participation rate."

What we've often failed to admit is that this phenomenon of remaining in school isn't particular to our generation. It's just what young workers do when they can't find work—for lack of other options, they try and improve their prospects, even where that may mean racking up further debt or student loans that will be deferred until professional employment comes along. So, to say Millennial employment is low because they're still going to school is like trying to say people can't afford medication because they're choosing to be poor. Millennials are continuing their education at an unusually high rate for their age group because they cannot find suitable work. And both these trends continue now, long after the Great Recession.[152] [153]

Finally, we come to the concept of the Millennial generation being the problem, as opposed to the possibility of them living within the problem. It's been said, repeatedly, that the narcissistic Millennial generation is the "Me Generation." Yet, in fact, the term "Me Generation" was dubbed in the 1970s to comment on the culture of narcissism among the younger generation of that era—namely, the Baby Boomers. It's inconsequential whether this began with the Boomers, and has continued in every subsequent generation, or whether it has always been the perception we cast on our youngest working generation. What matters is that this supposed narcissism has nothing to do with the soundness of our economy. Older generations see younger generations as lacking

---

152 Stephen Gandel, "OMG, Young Millennials Are the Job Market's Biggest Losers," *Fortune,* last modified March 4, 2016, http://fortune.com/2016/03/04/young-millennials-job-market-losers/.

153 Kelly Monahan, Jeff Schwartz, and Tiffany Schleeter, "Decoding Millennials in the Gig Economy," Deloitte Insights, last modified May 1, 2018, https://www2.deloitte.com/insights/us/en/focus/technology-and-the-future-of-work/millennials-in-the-gig-economy.html.

the work ethic they had, as being lazy or self-centered. It's part of a cycle we've seen for many generations now, and it's serving as a red herring to take us away from the actual issue.

Maybe we're blaming our lack of optimism for the future on a generation of Americans who, more than anything, are trying to figure out where our optimism originally came from while they watch their parents and each other work through underemployment, paycheck-to-paycheck living, and live with daily confusion with political leaders and media pundits claiming a healthy, rebounding economy, which makes each of us feel like we're the only one who is losing out.

Perhaps you're nodding your head along with me, or even shaking your head over this focus on a single generation, and you're wondering: *Brayden, why all this talk about Millennials? Really?* It's not because Millennials are special. It's only because we are the canary in the coal mine. Millennials are our sign of what's to come. And, on a larger scale, it's because it is the future of our economy we need to be most worried about.

According to Pew Research, Millennials have lower levels of employment than any of the last three recorded generations have had at their age; comparing the numbers shows that while the previous generation saw 78 percent of men and 69 percent of women employed, the Millennials' rates in 2014 were only 68 percent for men and 63 percent for women. When recalculated in 2018, the trend still continued with Millennial men having the lowest level of employment ever seen, ranging between 3 to 8 percent less, depending on the generation. Millennial women continued to fare better given social changes, but they're still 1 percent behind the last generation.[154] When you're talking about these kinds of systemic differences in our population, you're talking about a future with millions more headed to poverty. We are seeing a systemic shift that we haven't seen before, and it's something that we must be concerned about, given what our country now expects in the way of new job creation.

---

154   Fry, Igielnik, and Patten, "How Millennials Today Compare with Their Grandparents 50 Years Ago."

Twilight of the Idols

We don't like to talk about automation and AI, but again that factors here. Remember the Oxford University research that analyzed how susceptible jobs are to computerization, which found that 47 percent of the jobs in the U.S. are likely to disappear to automation in the next ten to twenty years? That will continue to impact these already record-low generational employment rates. Worse still, that does not even capture the larger issue. As costs continue to increase and wages continue to stagnant and decline, the human outcome is the ever-growing population living at subsistence or poverty wages. They don't pop up in the unemployment statistics, but they are the new casualty of this economic paradigm. As automation and AI continue to impact our future, this already unviable model will become increasingly unstable with each passing year.

Whether the challenges faced by automation will hit us harder in five years or in fifteen years, the fact is that we aren't ready to face such a giant shift in employment opportunities, and it's the hard-working people of this country who will suffer for it the most—not our leadership, or those stockholders who are already wealthy. It's going to be the middle class that is most significantly affected by automation and changes in technology as these factors eliminate jobs. The segment of our population that is critical to future stability and that is hanging on by a thread.

Complex issues like these aren't easy to deal with. They don't win campaigns. They aren't fun to talk about. Leadership can easily raise the donations and support they need by screaming about partisan social issues, but not bi-partisan economic solutions. The people who will be hurt aren't those people who are making the decisions or controlling purse strings for the government.

But we all have to accept that the forces of stagnant wages, exponential real expenses, systemic generational unemployment, and automation have the potential to destabilize our entire economy in a way that could diminish our economic and political leadership in the world. More importantly, these negative forces could hurt hundreds of millions of Americans.

Many people have argued that at every point in the past where advances in technology changed industry, we found a way to create as many jobs as we lost.[155] The changes in technology themselves brought about new jobs that couldn't have before been predicted. In fact, we have a long history proving this fact, so there must be nothing to worry about.

Well, maybe...but maybe not. There is a fundamental difference between this revolution and every prior technological revolution. This time, the revolution is based in human-level artificial intelligence. We are creating machines that will operate at the same level of intelligence humans have—within a ten to twenty year time frame. Machines that are able to self-replicate and make decisions.[156] The automobile created more jobs than it eliminated. But, the automobile couldn't make an automobile, or for that matter an assembly plant. This next generation of machines can.

Historically, higher productivity—that resulted due to the introduction of new technologies went hand in hand with job creation. That has changed in an unprecedented way.[157] It also used to be true that these same advances in productivity increased median family income, but in the '80s this pattern began to stutter, and for the last fifteen years it has been in full decline. Productivity has gone up, and GDP has gone up, but private employment and income have gone down. Chances are, you've seen this in your own family, whether via your very own bank account or those of your children and friends. It's gotten harder to survive, even as our technology and knowledge have progressed at an incredible pace; for most of us, smarter technology and advanced science

---

155 "What Can History Teach Us about Technology and Jobs?" McKinsey Global Institute, last modified February 2018, https://www.mckinsey.com/featured-insights/future-of-organizations-and-work/what-can-history-teach-us-about-technology-and-jobs.

156 David Rotman, "How Technology Is Destroying Jobs," *MIT Technology Review,* last modified June 12, 2013, https://www.technologyreview.com/s/515926/how-technology-is-destroying-jobs/.

157 Rotman, "How Technology Is Destroying Jobs."

haven't translated to greater surplus or financial security in our personal lives. And the trend is clear.

Will this trend turn around as technology advances? Will this technological process strengthen our middle class, as prior advances have?

Not within our current system. It doesn't take a fortune-teller to see that any gains that could be had will be felt only at the top, as our economic paradigm has systematically ensured for decades. The irony is that more surplus than ever is coming. Artificial intelligence and automation will likely mean more goods than we have today and more goods produced more easily than we probably need; in a system of economic inequality, however, our economy could still suffocate, no matter what size the surplus.

And that's what this comes down to. We can continue to watch this trend or we can reorganize our system.

I do have hope, but if that doesn't work, I also have a plan.

Let me start by repeating here that I'm a business owner. I'm an entrepreneur. I've also worked on economic legislation within my state, and I know what it takes to create change. Additionally, I grew up in a working-class family where my dad worked three jobs so that my mom could pursue her education. I grew up seeing their struggles and their work for a strong future, and learned to believe both in hard work and in the American Dream. And, I got to where I am now doing my best to help not just my family and my community, but our country. Given my background, I consider myself both pro-business and pro-worker. And, that's why I know there are mutual solutions to the issues we face.

I have firsthand experience with being unable to make ends meet. Even after getting my associate degree before graduating high school, overloading my classes, enrolling for summer quarter, getting a merit scholarship for two-thirds my tuition, working in the school cafeteria and graduating in eighteen months after high school, I graduated in debt just like everyone else. I started a business with no financial resources or connections. And, prior to raising funds everyone told me would be impossible to raise, I remember not having enough money in my bank account to buy a sandwich at Subway—an anniversary I celebrate every year on April 30th.

I have spent my entire career starting businesses, building entirely new inventions, and creating new jobs. Today, I own multiple businesses. I've worked on and helped pass successful economic legislation that I helped shape, prepped all the testimony for committee hearings, and helped organize the community to force legislators to support it. It's from this vantage point that I have perspective on how we rebuild our middle class.

If it is at all possible, and I have great hope it is, I want to build our economic paradigm to last when this upcoming disruption in jobs and economy happens. I want a tax code that benefits people who work for a living. I want every person in this country who wants to start a business and create jobs to get the chance. I want to see entrepreneurship taught in our core curriculum, I want there to be debt suspension for student loans if graduates want to start a company (since research shows us this is the #1 reason college graduates aren't starting companies today)[158], and I even want to push for tax refunds for early stage investors who help build our economic future, as is done in British Columbia[159] and the United Kingdom.[160] Everything we can do to foster entrepreneurship, small business, new business, and meaningful job creation in this country should be done. And, finally, through all of this, we must remember that every job we can save is a job earned, and we must

---

158   Bill Green, "Millennial Entrepreneurs Are Held Back Because of This 1 Reason," *Inc.*, last modified February 6, 2018, https://www.inc.com/bill-green/whats-holding-back-todays-millennial-entrepreneurs-and-what-they-need-to-succeed.html.

159   "Small Business Venture Capital Tax Credit," Government of British Columbia, accessed December 2, 2018, https://www2.gov.bc.ca/gov/content/taxes/income-taxes/corporate/credits/venture-capital.

160   "HS393 Seed Enterprise Investment Scheme - Income Tax and Capital Gains Tax Reliefs (2017)," GOV.UK, last modified April 9, 2018, https://www.gov.uk/government/publications/seed-enterprise-investment-scheme-income-tax-and-capital-gains-tax-reliefs-hs393-self-assessment-helpsheet/hs393-seed-enterprise-investment-scheme-income-tax-and-capital-gains-tax-reliefs-2017.

take every opportunity we can to create a meaningful job that will protect and strengthen the middle class.

Can I do this? No. Could the President do it? No. But could informed and organized American citizens make it happen? Absolutely. With a firm and consistent voice, we could.

These policies above could make a dramatic difference, even on their own, but they are only the tip of the iceberg. Electing, appointing, and hiring entrepreneurs throughout all reaches of government would create more opportunity to shift our system toward equality than I could ever hope to alone. They will have ideas far beyond what I could ever come up, because that is what entrepreneurs do—they have innovative ideas.

Successful entrepreneurs bring a lot to the table. They bring a willingness to move beyond the status quo and imagine how things can be restructured in a way that allows for change to happen. What's more, they bring with them a determination and optimism that thrives on growth, confidence in the American people, and plans for the future.

The real leaders we need are the few who, in spite of a system virtually eliminating the possibility of economic mobility, came from nothing. Leaders who still hold that close to their heart in an authentic way. Who understood what it took and how to make it possible for others.

It's important that our elected officials both understand our real economy today as it is felt by 99 percent of Americans and understand that our economy won't take care of itself. We need forward-thinking leaders and entrepreneurs who *get it*. Who understand what it takes to build something from nothing, and something better for our children.

Figuring out what to do if automation hits our country as hard as has been predicted is more difficult. Because it's true that even with a plan in place, we might not be able to change things as quickly as we need to at this point. It's just too many jobs. What if this revolution *is* unlike the ones that have come before it? What if we absolutely cannot create jobs as quickly as they go away in this era of human-level artificial intelligence?

Well, I have an answer for that, too, though at first consideration some might have a negative reaction. To those, I ask to suspend judgement until the full idea can be explained. If we want to maintain any semblance of our current economy and country, then we will need a program like Universal Basic Income.

Now, pause.

Breathe.

This is not socialism. A system of Universal Basic Income (UBI) would provide a minimum, livable income for those in the lower income brackets of our society. Those who found work would make more income, have more goods, live a higher quality of life than what they had before, and would also continue to be the middle class as we know it in the kind of capitalist society we have today. Those who competed for the scarcest of jobs or who ran the businesses themselves would continue to have significantly more wealth than the others. That's capitalism. This is just a new option, and one which we may have to consider if we want to continue moving forward through the type of upheaval that a drastic wave of job loss and change could create. It could also create a single point of focus upon which we could begin to decrease the spiraling economic inequality.

It's also not as significant of a jump as you might think. In fact, you might even just consider it a simplification of many of the programs we *already* have in place to tackle poverty in this country. Systems like social security to welfare to Medicaid that protect the most vulnerable in our society to keep our economic engine stable. In fact, eliminating a lot of the redundancy, administration, and bureaucracy of these current systems could actually save us a lot of money while simultaneously doing a better job at eliminating poverty.

Research even indicates a UBI of $1,000 per month could boost U.S. GDP by more than 12 percent over eight years.[161] If

---

161   Michalis Nikiforos, Marshall Steinbaum, and Gennaro Zezza, "Modeling the Macroeconomic Effects of a Universal Basic Income," Roosevelt Institute, last modified August 8, 2017, http://rooseveltinstitute.org/modeling-macroeconomic-effects-ubi/.

such a program becomes necessary, it would likely become an economic gain for our national economic growth.

Further, a 2017 study conducted by MIT that aggregated evidence from seven such social programs found them to have no effect on work behavior for men or women.[162] Yes, you read that right; despite social misconceptions, research shows us having access to social programs like UBI does not impact work behavior. People supported by these programs continued to work as they had before.

Now, if automation fundamentally displaces all of these jobs we're worrying about, then we can actually still rejoice. It means we will have more surplus of goods with fewer human workers than we have ever had in the past. As jobs are eliminated, we increase corporate taxes to compensate allowing corporations to slightly increase profits, rather than dramatically increase them. In that process, we fund our UBI program in addition to reallocating the budgets we already dedicate to social programs.

Our economic paradigm can shift into one that easily allows a system like UBI to exist—where all of our citizens find themselves able to have more than they did before, and where there are massive economic incentives for people to continue to compete for higher-paying jobs. Everyone will move into a higher quality of life, and we'll all be doing it together. There won't be the widening of the wealth gap or massive inflation, but a way forward that is actually built to satisfy each person's ambitions, talents, and needs so that we can grow as a country. Together.

It's still capitalism.

It's still the free market.

It's just a market adjusting to requiring less human labor than before.

Remember, nothing is set in stone, and we are at a point where we still have options: an alternative option could be reducing the work week to 25 or 30 hours. The last time we reduced it

---

162 Abhijit V. Banerjee et al., "Debunking the Stereotype of the Lazy Welfare Recipient."

was almost a century ago, in 1940, when a provision of the Fair Labor Standards Act mandated a 40-hour work week. It may have actually been famous American entrepreneur Henry Ford who have played a key role in transforming policy by shutting down his factories all of Saturday and Sunday starting in 1926. Even today, other industrialized countries in Europe have shorter work weeks. If our public policy can adapt even simple changes to accommodate economic equality in the age of automation and AI, then we actually have reason, dare I say it, for optimism.

A bolder effort on UBI or shorter work weeks doesn't need to be at the expense of the smaller goals laid out above that could help foster entrepreneurship and economic growth. We can go forward with a plan to boost our economy and our middle class with an economic paradigm built for progress and improvements to our status quo all at the same time. We can, and should, keep our eyes on these short-term goals with the hope that the upcoming revolution in automation and AI technologies will allow for as many jobs to be created as they destroy. And, meanwhile, just in case, we understand that the revolution might bring greater difficulties and change than we as a country have faced before when it comes to technological revolutions.

Our only potentially catastrophic impact will come from not preparing for the transition, and thus causing an economy on the verge of greater output than ever before to fail beyond any scale we have seen in the past. Consider that for a second. Our economy, with more output than ever, could fail as the result of growth. It's just that that growth would have been built with too few people behind it.

But, that's why we won't—why we can't—ignore the various paths on our horizon.

Instead, we need to start planning now.

As industries automate, we need to put tax structures in place that will level out corporate taxes with the jobs that are being lost; these revenues will fund programs that will support and re-train displaced workers in those same automating industries. This is a world where corporate profits can continue to increase gradually, while we also properly fund these critical programs—programs that will, on the whole, increase our economy, GDP, and the overall profit of those same corporations.

Those workers who we can re-train will then find new work. Those additional taxes, no longer needed to support those workers, can even further fund our UBI program. As funds become available, we can also shut down other redundant social programs, like food and housing subsidies that will become obsolete with UBI in place. And, over the coming years, we begin to build more and more resources designed to gently transition our economy into this new economic paradigm, even as we support entrepreneurship and pay down our national debt, all the while strengthening the middle class.

The truth is that this is more than possible. This process is going to unfold whether we like it or not. The question is just whether or not we prepare for it in time to participate in and shape it, or if we let these changes destabilize our future.

Chapter 11

Inequality for All

"First they came for the Socialists, and I did not speak out—
Because I was not a Socialist.

Then they came for the Trade Unionists, and I did not speak out—
Because I was not a Trade Unionist.

Then they came for the Jews, and I did not speak out—
Because I was not a Jew.

Then they came for me—and there was no one left to speak for me."

—Martin Niemöller

I'm going to draw a line right here. For a good portion of this country, the term *inequality* is a politically charged term for the left. A thinly veiled new name for the redistribution of wealth. It's so politically charged, in fact, that it tends to get ignored and thrown around in a way that allows for it to be nearly forgotten— mere political *white noise* spun up just to rally a few base votes before elections.

But, right here, right now, we're going to talk about the inequality which those on the right and the left completely agree on, and look at the pieces of this puzzle that just don't require any further debate—no matter what side you're on.

A question for you: Do children today have the same economic opportunity to be successful that they did twenty years ago? Assuming, of course, they're intelligent, innovative, hardworking, and have strong values and an education. If that's the case, then the answer is….

No, they don't.

Every American believes that children committed to hard work and an unwavering pursuit of the American Dream should earn their way to economic success in this country. We do vary on how we feel people become wealthy. Based on research conducted by Pew Research, 66 percent of Republicans feel it's due to hard work, while 60 percent of Democrats feel it's due to advantages early in life. And more than that, 56 percent of Republicans feel people become poor through a lack of effort, while 71 percent of Democrats feel people become poor through circumstances beyond their control.[163]

Yet, the divide in perception no longer matters. The quantitative results are in and it is a non-partisan issue that we all want our children to have the same chance the last generation did—and it is crystal clear that it is not happening.

And it's rapidly falling further away. Borrowing from my own personal experience, I know for a fact had I been born just five years later, I wouldn't own companies today. With the exact same effort, my student debt would have ended my journey before it had a chance to begin. This five year difference in time amounts to a $12,000–$17,000 difference in terms of tuition growth. In spite of my personal journey to afford my education, I stayed in the fight down to my last few dollars before getting the funding my business needed. With the additional debt, I would have had to quit working on my business idea long before I had any inclination

---

163 Samantha Smith, "Why People Are Rich and Poor: Republicans and Democrats Have Very Different Views," Pew Research Center, last modified May 2, 2017, http://www.pewresearch.org/fact-tank/2017/05/02/why-people-are-rich-and-poor-republicans-and-democrats-have-very-different-views/

we were going to get funded. I'd be working for someone else to start paying down that debt. This book wouldn't have been written. I wouldn't have had the ability to fight for the legislation I cared about or serve as a legislative action chair. I wouldn't have inventions and patents. My companies wouldn't have started. Our products wouldn't be helping tens of thousands of students.

But, this is the world our children live in, and each year, fewer and fewer will have a shot at their dreams. No matter how hard they work. That's why I am in this fight. I know the difference it made for me, and the hairbreadth away it was from never happening.

So, what do we do to make sure kids today have the same economic opportunity as they did twenty years ago, and twenty years before that?

For now, it seems, we argue about it and get nowhere. The Democratic Party recently unveiled their plan, A Better Deal.[164] It discusses inequality and a crackdown on the abuse of corporate and political power. The problem? There isn't much it doesn't mention. It's a kitchen-sink approach that even includes some of Trump's campaign messaging. What it does say is *minimalist*, not *radical*, and comes from a group of leaders who've been making all the decisions that have spun this inequality out of control.[165] It's hard to believe those that have brought us here want to take us somewhere else. Where are the bold, new voices that are laser-focused on solving the greatest economic challenges of our time?

Unfortunately, the Republican Party's deal isn't any better. It's just more straightforward. Their tax proposals outright and unapologetically say, *we're working for the consolidating moneyed interests*.

The problem is both sides are.

---

164 "The Proposals," A Better Deal, accessed December 2, 2018, https://abetterdeal. democraticleader.gov/category/the-proposals/.

165 Darrell Delamaide, "Opinion: The Democrats' 'Better Deal' Is a Box-Office Dud," MarketWatch, last modified July 25, 2017, https://www.marketwatch.com/story/the-democrats-better-deal-is-a-box-office-dud-2017-07-25.

Twilight of the Idols

As one of the other 99 percent of Americans, your choices right now are to vote for someone who is candidly working against your interests, or vote for someone who is unofficially working against your interests. It's simply a fact that this consolidation has happened like clockwork under both parties, regardless of congressional makeup or executive branch.

It's time for simplified plans. For transparency and track records. Any deal that is based on more than one central issue becomes an unprecedentedly difficult, partisan debate, and in a special interest-driven Congress, the deal isn't going to happen. You can't prioritize everything, and in a world where our government struggles to get anything done, we can't afford the distraction.

In business, and government, those that win tackle the issue that makes everything else easier, or irrelevant, and today that is economic inequality.

Almost all of the major political issues of our time are effects caused by inequality. It's just going to take leadership with enough courage to risk their jobs. It's an issue without major PACs and donors. An issue that won't be supported by the major parties. An issue that, frankly, will get you fired. But, an issue, nonetheless, that will give the children and grandchildren in this country a future.

The Environment: The poorest, both globally and nationally, are being impacted first by environmental degradation. The wealthy don't live near the trash dumps. The poor can't afford rising food prices for organic produce. You can pay to distance yourself from these problems—for now. If the wealthiest among us were being impacted on a personal level right now, you would see unprecedented action toward solving climate change and creating clean energy jobs of the future.

Immigration: Ask the majority of those in support of closing our borders to immigrants and they'll talk about how immigrants are taking our jobs and closing our factories. In reality, our factories are not being closed because of immigrants, the Chinese, or any other people, but because of automation. Yes, globalization plays a role, but machines will continue to take more of those jobs than people.

Nonetheless, it's economic inequality and the ever-growing wage gap that is driving many people to support anti-immigrant policies—they're told that closing our borders and introducing tariffs will save their jobs. People in a precarious financial position will support almost anything to protect their family.

Healthcare: We can't pass legislation that would both save taxpayer dollars and provide everyone in our country with health care access: why? Because an oligopoly of wealthy insurance companies like things the way they are. And, they can afford the Congressmen on either side to back that up.

The War on Drugs: Today, we've watched a national epidemic emerge that rises steadily year after year. Heroin addiction is three times more likely in those who make less than $20,000 a year than those who make $50,000 or more. Research also indicates that a country with a healthy middle class and low or moderate levels of economic inequality see lower addiction rates with most kicking their addiction by age 30.[166]

Mass Incarceration: Economic inequality is directly correlated to crime. It's why incarcerated people have a median annual income of $19,185 prior to their incarceration, which is 41 percent less than non-incarcerated people of similar ages.[167] We've privatized prisons, increased mandatory minimums, and filled our prisons at twice the rate of any other modern country. We've then set up the poorest of the poor to work for pennies or nothing to support some of the most successful companies in

---

166   Szalavitz, "Addictions Are Harder to Kick When You're Poor. Here's Why."

167   Rabuy and Kopf. "Prisons of Poverty."

our country, from Whole Foods[168] to McDonald's,[169] Victoria's Secret,[170] to Wal-Mart.[171]

We're no longer guided by the invisible hand of capitalism, but the silent hands of monopolies and a political establishment that is far too cozy with them. It's this relationship that has slowly, but inevitably, led to the number of publicly traded companies to drop in half over the last twenty years. We're talking about numbers that illustrate a difference of more than one thousand companies lower than what we saw in 1975.[172]

Debt: If we wanted to strip free markets and capitalism away, and replace it with a class system ensuring the failure of equal opportunity for hardworking Americans, then we would need to bake institutionalized debt into the system. It would have to exist in areas that every American depends on, and it would have to ensure a cycle of debt.

And, we've done exactly that.

Housing has always been an institution that has helped build middle-class wealth, savings, and retirement. Today, for one simple reason, it's become a chasm, helping build the acceleration of wealth to the rich and pushing the newest middleclass adults toward poverty.

---

168   Allison Aubrey, "Whole Foods Says It Will Stop Selling Foods Made with Prison Labor," *NPR,* last modified September 30, 2015, https://www.npr.org/sections/thesalt/2015/09/30/444797169/whole-foods-says-it-will-stop-selling-foods-made-by-prisoners

169   Sara Flounders, "The Pentagon and Slave Labor in U.S. Prisons," Global Research, last modified September 1, 2018, http://www.globalresearch.ca/the-pentagon-and-slave-labor-in-u-s-prisons/25376.

170   Caroline Winter, "What Do Prisoners Make for Victoria's Secret?" *Mother Jones,* last modified August 2008, https://www.motherjones.com/politics/2008/07/what-do-prisoners-make-victorias-secret/.

171   Victoria Law, "Martori Farms: Abusive Conditions at a Key Wal-Mart Supplier," Truthout, last modified June 24, 2011, https://truthout.org/articles/martori-farms-abusive-conditions-at-a-key-walmart-supplier/.

172   Barry Ritholtz, "Where Have All the Public Companies Gone?" Bloomberg, last modified June 24, 2015, https://www.bloomberg.com/view/articles/2015-06-24/where-have-all-the-publicly-traded-companies-gone-.

The reason is emerging American families are burdened with systemic debt—not assets. That is why fewer Americans than ever in our emerging generation are buying homes—doing so at less than half the rate seen in China. The accelerating cost of housing, and the barrier of down payments, are leaving many of us paying more in rent than we would on mortgages, further accelerating the wealth transfer. We just can't ever save enough to get to the other side. Rents go up, we struggle to meet them, and any savings we might have scraped together for a down payment go to rent or some emergency that pops up. It's an endless cycle, but the slower this generation transitions into homeownership, the more we'll see that wealth is being *irrevocably* transferred from the lower class to the upper class.

Education has also always remained a staple of stability for the American middle class. Investment in an education leads to higher wages throughout a lifetime, but today the cost of that education leads to decades of indebtedness for most.

The next generation of middle-class Americans is trapped. To get an education, they must amass significant debt. Then, they will pay rents higher than mortgages for decades afterward, while they try to pay down debt and put together enough savings for a down payment. All the while, they'll be losing out on decades of savings that could have gone toward their retirement. This same future middle class is experiencing lower levels of employment than any of our recorded generations (excluding women during generations when they couldn't or were encouraged not to work).[173] We are seeing the rise of the gig economy and a historically unprecedented separation between productivity (output) and compensation (wages).[174] Access to global trade has brought an enormous supply of low-level and high-skilled workers to our doorstep, with more $1 per day wage earners *and* genius-level employees in China than there are overall people in the United States.

---

173   Fry, Igielnik, and Patten, "How Millennials Today Compare with Their Grandparents 50 Years Ago."

174   "The Productivity–Pay Gap."

Twilight of the Idols

We are simultaneously seeing the elimination of jobs at a similarly unheard-of rate[175] and are at risk of seeing almost 50 percent of all current jobs disappear within the next fifteen years, with automation replacing low-level workers and AI replacing high-skilled workers.

But the single worst fact of all is this one: If wealth accumulates faster than economies can grow, then you'll make more money being wealthy, and not working, than being middle class and working. Let me put that another way. Not only are those born with wealth being born on third base. They're born running faster. In short, they can make more money speculating on the economy than participating in it.

Are there exceptions? Absolutely. You can win the lottery or a few people might slip through the cracks. But that's true in any class system and, as Americans, these exceptions don't help the 99.99 percent of families that will live by the rules we build our economy on.

Sadly, new comprehensive data has been released to show that this is, in fact, exactly what is happening: Wealth accumulates faster—much faster—than the economy can keep up to. This means that in coming years, wealth inequality is likely to accelerate if we do not take action. Inaction alone will ensure the results we cannot survive. [176]

If the political will existed, our tax system could reward hard work over wealth in a heartbeat, but today, returns on investments are taxed at about half the rate as hard-earned income.

Housing, higher education, and taxes have become central pieces of our infrastructure that are ensuring an ever-accelerated transfer of wealth from the working poor to the upper class. In turn, this inequality becomes the root cause driving our political divisions, from health care, to immigration and jobs, to the environment. But, with all of the problems, we talk about the

---

175   Frey and Osborne, "The Future of Employment."

176   Ingraham, "Massive New Data Set Suggests Economic Inequality is About to Get Even Worse."

symptoms rather than the root cause that's driving them. A cause we actually agree on: that our children should have the same opportunity *or better* to succeed than we did.

Let me be clear in saying that I am not belittling the importance and value of these political issues. As well as many other issues of social fairness, fiscal conservation, and civil liberties that I've not discussed in this chapter, or even this book. It's not either-or. It's *both-and*. The point is that by focusing *just* on economic inequality we could, as a consequence, solve a great many of these other issues in ways both the left and right would support. For instance, making health care more affordable and accessible to individuals and less expensive on taxpayers.

Many of these divisive issues might just resolve themselves.

If you have more than $1,000 in savings right now, as I said earlier, you are one of the lucky ones who are living in the top 40 percent.[177] It's time to act while you still have a voice to do so; with every passing year, more of us will be struggling for basic survival. We have to act while we have the time, and what amounts to the luxury, to do so—or, we'll fail. As individuals and as a nation.

If you still hold any hope that our current Congress, or political structure, will solve these problems without our intervention and active demands for them to do so, then let me remind you that we now have the oldest Congress in U.S. history.[178] Our Congressional leaders have been there almost as long as these issues have been developing and both sides have overseen its development during different administrations. If they were going to fix the problems for us, they would have done so by now.

The good news is that we, the people, have a viable, credible chance at reform. A chance I will describe in the final chapter.

---

177   Quentin Fottrell, "Most Americans Have Less Than $1,000 in Savings," MarketWatch, last modified December 23, 2015, https://www.marketwatch.com/story/most-americans-have-less-than-1000-in-savings-2015-10-06.

178   "The 115th Congress Is among the Oldest in History," Quorum, accessed December 2, 2018, https://www.quorum.us/data-driven-insights/the-115th-congress-is-among-the-oldest-in-history/175/.

Chapter 12

Of the People, By the People, For the People

If you're anything like me, you read through these chapters with an almost familiar, intuitive understanding. You already knew so many of these changes had happened or were happening around you. Yet, now, confronted with everything that's been spelled out in black and white, you feel compelled to *do* something, but maybe you aren't sure what.

This isn't an intellectual exercise for you. Day in and day out, you may feel anger, fear, hopelessness, shame, or confusion—but you still love this country. You still love it because, deep down, you still want to give of yourself to make it better. It's your home, and the place where you want to be successful, safe, and fulfilled, along with your family and your neighbors and your friends. If you're like me, you still have some optimism that we're not done being great. As with our grandparents, it is this unspoken culture of belief that can give us a new hope.

Before I tell you what you can do, let's tackle the counterargument. This time, that counterargument comes from within—and it is within each of us.

Imagine having your daughter, nephew, spouse, or someone who you care for look up at you, eyes filled with emotion and anger, to say, *You have the privilege and influence to make a difference, but the world isn't going to change because you aren't part of the solution.*

Brayden W.B. Olson

This happened to me. It came from someone important to my life who studies and researches political violence and oppression. Who at the time was dedicating her life to combating child sex trafficking in Seattle. And in that moment, I froze. The person speaking to me listed off the many positions of influence I held: as a business owner, a Congressional candidate, a white male, someone with media access, and a person of youth and energy. It dawned on me as they were speaking that I too felt powerless.

As she listed each of these areas of influence I thought, *Yeah, but...my youth discounts my experience, my gender and race don't define my ideas, I only run small businesses, and as a candidate, I have even less credibility and no one believes anything I say to be genuine.* My excuses went on. Anyone's excuses could go on, and on, because it's easier to make excuses than to live day by day with the consequences of speaking out—or trying to help and failing publicly. I felt completely powerless in that moment—and yet, that was my greatest mistake.

Powers far beyond me may have forced my withdrawal as a candidate without contest, but that doesn't mean we stop fighting. That is why I wrote this book. I may never be in a position to help solve these problems, but I will never waste one breath from trying to be part of the solution.

I bet you feel powerless, too. Your positions might be different. Your excuses might be different. Maybe you're retired (so you have free time, but no one listens to you). Or, you're a middle manager at a big company (where you have thousands of co-workers around you, but you're not the boss). Or, you're assistant pastor at your church (where hundreds look to you for guidance, but you aren't allowed to talk about politics). Or a reporter (who writes for a newspaper, but feels they need to keep their head down to keep their job). Maybe you're a woman (so now is the best time ever in this country to run for office, but we've never elected a female President). Or, you're a minority (who has a political microphone right now, but fears anger and retribution from those who don't share your identity).

Twilight of the Idols

I feel powerless too.

But this isn't my story. It's yours.

And it's not just yours, it's ours. No one leader can fix our country. Nor can any one leader break it. No one party can fix our country, nor can any one party break it.

Put the excuses out of the way. Tell that little negative voice in your head to stop lying to you. You are only powerless if you do nothing. You could read this book, shake your head at the sad situation we're in, and forget about it—moving on with only the hope that someone else will listen, someone else will lead us out of this crisis and do something to change things.

But you are only powerless if you do nothing.

If you take *one action*, and persist with that action, you are powerful. If you stay in the fight, you'll inspire others. You'll see one become two and two become hundreds.

Here is the bottom line. There are two forces of power in an economy: wealth and production, capital and labor. Put another way, the interests of money and the interests of the people. Together, we build the world, but every civilization that has gone too far out of balance has collapsed.

Now, we were created to be a government of the people, by the people, and for the people as Lincoln once said. The problem is that we are no longer that government. And we are no longer acting like the people that choose such a government as our forefathers imagined and worked so hard to create. Instead, we've created the government we deserve through our inaction. Instead, we've been accepting the status quo of economic inequality. Many of us have given up the belief that real, systemic change can happen. Though it was not that long ago in this country that it did. Our challenge, as a people, is to take back our government by renewing in ourselves that attitude we once had as a nation, remembering: "Of the People, By the People, For the People." We are that people, and we've been powerful in every generation that has come before.

So, let's look at how to take back the control we've lost.

First, it's important to understand that 91 percent of races are determined by who raises the most funding.[179]

After the 2010 Citizens United decision that allowed corporations to more directly engage in swaying election outcomes, the amount of independent expenditures (funds spent by billionaires and corporations) grew from about $191 million in 2010 to about $1.55 billion in 2016, representing an *eight-fold* increase. At the same time, voter turnout plummeted. In fact, fewer people voted in their 2014 Senate races than at any time since 1990, despite there being a higher population.[180] In 2012, 67 percent of all campaign funding came from big donors and Political Action Committee (PACs).[181] When you hear the term, *Political Action Committee*, think, *pooled special interest money*. In 2014, PACs and big money donors were 80 percent of campaign funding.[182] The American people are playing an ever smaller role in our government, cycle by cycle.

In short, 91 percent of elections are decided by independent expenditures (IEs), PACs, and large donors. That's the bottom line. Once elected, incumbency is so strong that even though Americans' confidence in Congress hit *an all time, historical rock bottom of just 7 percent in 2015*, we still saw 98 percent of the House and 93 percent of the Senate re-elected in 2016.[183] [184]

---

179 Lowery, "91% of the Time the Better-Financed Candidate Wins. Don't Act Surprised."

180 Desilver and Van Kessel, "As More Money Flows into Campaigns, Americans Worry about Its Influence."

181 *Money Wins Congressional Races 91% of the Time,* 2012, Represent.us, https://visual.ly/community/infographic/politics/how-money-won-congress.

182 *Money Still Wins 91% of Congressional Races,* 2014, Represent.us, http://bulletin.represent.us/wp-content/uploads/sites/3/2015/10/MoneyWinsCongress14_C.gif.

183 Kyle Kondik and Geoffrey Skelley, "Incumbent Reelection Rates Higher than Average in 2016," University of Virginia Center for Politics, last modified December 15th, 2016, http://www.centerforpolitics.org/crystalball/articles/incumbent-reelection-rates-higher-than-average-in-2016/.

184 Rebecca Riffkin, "Public Faith in Congress Falls Again, Hits Historic Low," Gallup, last modified June 19, 2014, http://news.gallup.com/poll/171710/public-faith-congress-falls-again-hits-historic-low.aspx.

Twilight of the Idols

The people have completely lost control of the government. That control has been given, instead, to the ever shrinking list of the few who control the wealth.

In the past, organizations of people would band together to help inform members of the community about which candidates best represented them. Yet, even in my own Congressional race experience, I personally witnessed that many associations and unions would endorse candidates without even conducting interviews or sending questionnaires to consider their stance on the issues they care about. They would merely endorse whatever candidate they were told to endorse by party bosses, without thought to what views the candidate they were endorsing held and whether there were choices that better represented their membership. If even our smallest, grassroots organizations no longer act on the interests of the people, then who does?

An overwhelming majority of both Democrat and Republican voters want Congress to work to reduce the influence of money in politics, according to an Ipsos poll.[185] Americans are totally aligned on this. What most of them don't know, or understand, is that it is possible. In fact, it wasn't that long ago that we had better checks and balances in play.

If we want to rebalance the power in this country, we need to give power back to the people when it comes to how our representation is chosen. We need to have a system that incentivizes the behavior we want to see in our representatives and government, as opposed to the behavior we have now.

To do so, we need to change three things:

1) *We need to establish term limits.* A federal representative may serve twelve years total in either the House or the Senate. If we made this change, in one sweeping motion, no one in our Congress could be much more than a decade removed from being part of their community once again. Rather than having detached

---

185 Daniel Hensel, "New Poll Shows Money in Politics Is a Top Voting Concern," Issue One, last modified June 29, 2016, https://www.issueone.org/new-poll-shows-money-in-politics-is-a-top-voting-concern/.

representatives, we would bring D.C. into our backyards once again with representatives who have lived, and will live again soon, within their communities. Whatever decisions they make, good or bad, will have much more immediate, personal consequences. We reframe the entire endeavor from being a lucrative career to being a period of public service, as it once was.

With this change, we will also send significantly more new voices, ideas, opinions, and backgrounds to Congress during the same periods of time. Simply put, more of us will go to Congress, and that means more families and communities will participate in our government. And, incumbency will influence far fewer elections in this country.

2) *We need to get money out of politics.* Both independent expenditures and political action committees should be eliminated. The only advertisements for or against a political candidate will come from a candidate's campaign. The only contributions to a campaign will come from individual, real human donors. Plain and simple.

In addition to ensuring that election funding is determined by real people, there is another immediate benefit. In a heartbeat, we eliminate dirty political attack ads. It's tougher to spread dirt when you've got to put your own name on it. If there is a real public concern, then the public will appreciate your bringing it to their attention. If it is just dirty politics, the public will respond in kind.

Finally, many states have set maximum limits on how much campaigns can raise. We need to elevate these to the federal level. We put a $1M ceiling on every Congressional campaign. $2M on every Senate campaign. $50M for Presidential campaigns. Not one dollar more can be spent by anyone—even out of their own pocket. Campaigns will be won by the quality of your ideas, because every credible federal candidate will quickly raise their maximum campaign limit. You can out-think your opponent, but you can't outspend them.

3) *We need real public oversight into Congressional ethics.* If we fix the entire system, there is one final *gotcha*. Corporations and special interests can't help you with your re-election. They can't give you enough money to outspend your opponent. They can't directly write you a check.... But, what about job offers when your service is over? If you just vote *yes* on the bills they need passed? Or, a $300K check to come speak at an executive luncheon? Members of Congress should be required to privately turn over their family finances to an ethics committee after their retirement. These finances would stay private and be kept within the committee, but the committees will elect one citizen of each state to review these records every two years. The sole purpose of this committee is to eliminate the loopholes. Our members of Congress won't be influenced by anyone beyond their own conscience and the people in their communities they will go back home to in no more than one future term.

With these simple changes, the people will recover their government, candidates will be elected again based on the quality of their ideas, and corporations won't be able to run Congress. Perhaps most importantly, our Congress can actually do its job. As a candidate, the first thing you are told is that you will now be spending 80 percent of your time on calls raising money. Once elected, you're told to expect to continue spending 50 percent of your time on calls raising money. Everyone, either inside or outside of the system, will tell you how absurd this. The changes we're talking about here will put Congress back to work as legislators, not fundraisers, which almost every true public servant would be overjoyed to have happen.

You may be nodding in agreement with everything I just said, and yet believe none of these changes are possible. I understand. We've been conditioned to believe that. Conditioned to believe it in spite of the fact that just generations ago the people of our country rose up to demand seemingly far more impossible things from their govern—from Women's Suffrage to Civil Rights.

The good news is we do have such mechanisms. Our country's founders ensured that Congress always had a check, should they become too powerful. I'm speaking of an Article 5 Convention of States. However, before we get into that let's discuss our other options.

An Article 5 Convention is a powerful mechanism that I believe in, but it is not without risk. Prior to that becoming our best option, if it were possible for a responsible voting public to put our country over party and self in the coming years we could vote for candidates and initiatives that promise and commit themselves to term limits, campaign finance reform and create public oversight into Congressional finances.

This could be possible if a known, bi-partisan, trusted source of news emerged that could directly engage and inform the public in a way that began to shift election outcomes *in spite of* funds raised or incumbency. This alone could push the aforementioned three critical reforms and others such as ending gerrymandering, enabling rank choice voting, and increasing voting rights and access. In short, piece by piece, getting more and more power back into the hands of informed voters.

Our second possible solution, as improbable as it might seem as an outsider, is that there are some efforts underway in Congress today to change the rules and procedures. Ending pay-to-play chairmanships and replacing them with merit selection, reigning in leadership PACS, and establishing term limits. Further, distributing the appropriations responsibility more equitably across all members of the House, rather than just a handful of ordained leaders. All this and even the revolutionary idea of giving legislators enough time to actually read the legislation they are voting on, which is unbelievably not current standard practice. Rather, they're simply told by the aids of party bosses whether to vote "yes" or "no," and not giving time to read critical legislation only further empowers this kind of manipulation.

To be clear, I would prefer these more conservative options. However, any route, whether by Congressional reform or an organized, informed electorate that didn't address term limits, campaign finance reform, and public oversight into Congressional finances as proposed would fall short of restoring meaningful democracy to our political system.

Once more, no country can sustain itself for long without collapse or revolution with the kind of economic inequality we now experience. Simply put, most Americans will now spend their lives in debt slowly paying their earnings up to wealthy shareholders who take ever greater pieces of the output of their labor, because we can no longer afford food, shelter, education, medicine, and our basic modern needs without this debt infrastructure. We are running out of time.

For this reason, we must pursue these reforms and an Article 5 convention simultaneously. If we do not see meaningful progress in the next few years, then I believe our last peaceful and positive hope is the Convention of States. If we don't see progress, then we need to take the convention through to conclusion. There are multiple movements underway now to enact an Article 5 Convention of States to amend our Constitution, with 28 states[186] and millions of people behind it. The largest movement is a conservative one, but there are liberal movements as well. Article 5 was our Founding Fathers' way of trying to provide protections to the people for the day when the Federal government might lose its way.

For those unfamiliar with an Article 5 convention, please know I will address it in detail after a few words for those who are more familiar with it.

Depending on who you are, an Article 5 convention might be the most controversial thing I have written about so far in this book. Reading some of the internet articles, this movement is being portrayed by many as the scariest thing that could happen to our country. And, for the established interests, I imagine it might be.

For the American people, I'll put it plainly. I believe a big risk is better than a certain, slow collapse.

---

186 "U.S. Constitution Threatened as Article V Convention Movement Nears Success," Common Cause, last modified September 2018, https://www.commoncause.org/wp-content/uploads/2018/09/Article-V-Memo-Sept-2018.pdf.

Brayden W.B. Olson

To be clear, I don't think we even have to hold a convention. Congress has the capacity to make the changes we want. We simply need to show them that if they don't, a Convention will take place to ensure these changes will happen. That would be enough to force the change on Congress, Convention or not.

Do the current movements cover everything they should cover? No. Is this path perfect? No. Is it something to be treated with great caution? Yes.

As we go down this path, we need the states passing these votes to support a convention to also establish ground rules in the votes they are passing. Their vote of support should also add guidance to how the Convention of States will be conducted, most notably keeping the reforms to only a handful of bi-partisan key issues that can be broadly supported by our country, like budget, debt, campaign finance reform, term limits, and public oversight into Congressional ethics and finances. Many of these are already the focus points of the various movements.

This movement is exciting, and has great potential, but I only see it as a catalyst for awakening our newest generation of political activists. If we want any chance at putting enough pressure on our government to make the kinds of changes discussed in this chapter, then we are going to have to step up and organize like prior generations did for Civil Rights and Women's Suffrage. The alternative is to watch our ideals, like being the land of opportunity in the world, slip through our fingers.

Let me explain about the convention process itself.

In short, each state can file (through either initiative or legislature) for a Convention of States. If two-thirds (34) states call for one, we're able to form a Constitutional Convention in order to directly amend the Constitution. Each state sends a representative (one person) to this convention, and whatever is decided by a majority there is then proposed for ratification by the states themselves. If a three-quarters majority (38) of the legislatures approve, we could establish term limits, campaign finance reform, and ethical oversight as part of an updated Constitution.

By no means would this be simple. It would be the defining moment in the political activism of a generation, but this process could bring these issues to a head. It could be the mechanism that would drive the American people to the level of activism required to demand these changes. It would be the Millennial Generation's issue at the scale of Civil Rights.

At first blush, I know this sounds hard to grasp. It hasn't been used before, after all. Amending the Constitution is crazy, right?

But, as of the writing of this book, 28 states have already called for one. 28 states have already called for a Convention of States. In the last eight years, fifteen states have joined the movement. Based on an analysis of the remaining legislatures, pundits believe this could feasibly happen by 2019, when Montana's legislature gets back in session though it could also likely take a few more years to gather the necessary states. Much of this movement has been driven by a small, shoestring organization called Balanced Budget Amendment Task Force (BBATF) that received just under $50,000 in donations in 2015.[187]

At this moment, the outspoken National Taxpayers' Union, which has long advocated for this convention, *and* the well-known government reform organization, Common Cause, which is fiercely opposed to this convention, both put the probability of a 2020 convention at the same likelihood: 50/50.[188]

Now, a well-funded and credible, but right-leaning, Convention of States group has swooped in to push the momentum forward. Their focus is a balanced budget amendment. They want to reign in the power of the federal government, institute term limits, and reduce taxes among other things. It's a part of the picture, but we need an equally well-funded and credible left-leaning organization to balance the narrative so that we can represent a package for all

---

187 "America Might See a New Constitutional Convention in a Few Years," *The Economist*, last modified September 30, 2017, https://www.economist.com/briefing/2017/09/30/america-might-see-a-new-constitutional-convention-in-a-few-years.

188 "America Might See a New Constitutional Convention in a Few Years."

Americans—one that includes the campaign finance reform and congressional ethics oversight discussed earlier.

In the past, support for this mechanism has been successfully used to put enough pressure on Congress to force change. It's time to do that again. If we organize for a convention that *will* make the above three amendments, then, at any point before we have to convene the convention, we can and will gladly accept Congress simply putting these system checks in place. All three of them. If not, we, the people, hold our convention.

The fear mongers, and virtually every federal official who likes the way things operate now, say such a convention will go awry. They could do *anything* in this convention—that's the way their argument goes. The conveners could ban children from candy stores! They could shut down public schools or raise taxes at will! They could *hurt* the middle class!

But, that isn't how it would work.

The convention *could* do anything, yes, but only so long as 38 states would approve it. Nothing that leans too far to the left or right will be ratified by 38 states, nor the populations of 38 states. But the issues we're talking about would get voted into action because they have across-the-board support from average Americans. Such a convention would enact term limits. Campaign reform. Congressional oversight. Issues that the American people are overwhelmingly united in supporting.

82 percent of us want term limits.[189] 77 percent of us support campaign finance reform.[190] These are non-partisan issues that the people of our country would vote for without a second thought. That is why our Founders gave us this option for when our Representatives no longer represented us.

You might ask, then, *Why just these three changes? There is so much more that needs to be fixed!* Simple. We need these

---

189 McLaughlin and Davin, "M&A Poll."

190 Bradley Jones, "Most Americans Want to Limit Campaign Spending, Say Big Donors Have Greater Political Influence," Pew Research Center, last modified May 8, 2018, http://www.pewresearch.org/fact-tank/2018/05/08/most-americans-want-to-limit-campaign-spending-say-big-donors-have-greater-political-influence/.

three changes because our system of government isn't working as it should. We must tackle these first, because a functioning government can and will fix all the other issues. How our representation is elected is centrally important, and a sign our democratic process is working, or not. The rest will quite literally take care of itself with the right leadership in place. If we get the right people, with the right motivations, then any other change we need will come thereafter.

Trying to do more could get in the way of the movement as a whole.

The second big argument we often hear is that we no longer have any James Madisons or Thomas Jeffersons to govern such a convention. While that isn't true, I don't debate the fact that they're harder to find these days. Nor that they're even harder to find among our elected officials.

So, if you want to send a Madison or a Jefferson, who do we send? Our governors? Our senators? Not in my opinion.

Remember: our Founding Fathers were among the young, independently minded adults of their generation, and that is what we need again. When we signed the Declaration of Independence, the Father of the Constitution, the Father of what became the Republican Party, and the Father of what became the Democratic Party were 25, 21, and 33 respectively.[191] That's right—Madison was 25, Hamilton was 21, and Jefferson was 33. Now, it is true that they worked in conjunction with great leaders like Benjamin Franklin, who was 70 at the time, and that is critical, too. However, if our Founding Fathers felt about their youth the way our political system thinks about our youth today, then Madison, Hamilton, and Jefferson wouldn't have been there. They were, essentially, the Millennial generation of the time.

Instead, let's send some of our idealistic, independent-minded adults who are in their 20s and 30s and who find themselves in the

---

191 Todd Andrlik, "How Old Were the Leaders of the American Revolution on July 4, 1776?" *Slate Magazine,* last modified August 20, 2013, http://www.slate.com/articles/news_and_politics/politics/2013/08/how_old_were_the_founding_father_the_leaders_of_the_american_revolution.html.

thick of all of the problems our system has allowed to snowball. Much like the original Jefferson and Madison.

Should we only send our young adults? Of course not. Nor did our Forefathers who had the steady, seasoned hands of George Washington and Benjamin Franklin. Yet, our representation should look like the population of this country. Ultimately, the consequences of these decisions will be most greatly felt by our Millennial generation and those behind us—whatever those consequences are.

Nearly 50 percent of Millennials are political independents, which has grown by 22 percent since 2004, and is the highest level of political dissatisfaction Pew Research has seen for any generation in the decades they have conducted this polling.[192] [193] We grew up witnessing the result of partisanship, and we want real change. We've been fooled once or twice, but with each cycle, fewer of us are being fooled—and the consequences of today's political inaction have life and death consequences for us.

This mentality creates an immense opportunity—an opportunity not just for Millennials, but for all the common sense Americans who have been waiting for a breakthrough in an ever growing partisan divide. It's a movement for Boomers, Xers, and everyone in between who also want to see this independent mentality take hold.

Together, we could begin to organize such groups in all 50 states to support the Article 5 movement, to hold it accountable and to demand successful ratification.

So what could you do, right now? It starts with a small step. Reach out. Left, right, and center—we could all organize around these three principle changes, but we can't include you if we don't know you are out there.

---

192 Natalie Villacorta, "Poll: Half of Millennials Independent," *The Politico*, last modified March 7, 2014, https://www.politico.com/story/2014/03/millennials-independence-poll-104401.

193 Peter Levine, "The Waning Influence of American Political Parties," The Conversation, last modified March 31, 2016, https://theconversation.com/the-waning-influence-of-american-political-parties-56875.

Twilight of the Idols

Such movements of the people have proved greatly successful before. Just before the turn of the twentieth century, the Progressive Party Movement elected eight governors and forty-five members of U.S. Congress and drove changes we still feel today, from graduated income tax to the beginning of public transit. Later, in 1912, the Progressive Party pushed issues like an eight-hour workday, social security, and much more. We are cut from the same cloth as these bold Americans. All you need is to take the first step: join in.

Join a movement local to you that supports the Convention of States. Or, connect at *www.therebellionapp.com* and we will help you find one. Or, write me. If there was anything in this book that resonated with your story or that you have an example of, tell me. If there was an idea that inspired you or helped clarify something you now better understand, let me know. I plan to share these thoughts and letters publicly so that we can all see, left and right, that we are not alone.

We are in the twilight of so many of the idols, beliefs, ideas, and values that we hold about our country. And as a people, we only have a few options in front of us. We can watch our society fall into disrepair, exhibiting further inequality every year until the house of cards eventually collapses. Or, if we believe in our country and our people still, we can start a peaceful and loud rebellion. A new hope for our next generation.

I choose the latter option, but this isn't my American story. It's yours.

Epilogue

"Can you say why America is the greatest country in the world?

"It's not the greatest country in the world. That's my answer... there's absolutely no evidence to support the statement that we're the greatest country in the world. We're 7th in literacy, 27th in math, 22nd in science, 49th in life expectancy, 178th in infant mortality, 3rd in median household income, number 4 in labor force and number 4 in exports. We lead the world in only three categories: number of incarcerated citizens per capita, number of adults who believe angels are real and defense spending, where we spend more than the next 26 countries combined, 25 of whom are allies. So when you ask what makes us the greatest country in the world, I don't know what the fuck you're talking about! Yosemite?!

"It sure used to be.... We stood up for what was right. We fought for moral reason. We passed laws, struck down laws, for moral reason. We waged wars on poverty, not on poor people. We sacrificed, we cared about our neighbors, we put our money where our mouths were and we never beat our chest. We built great, big things, made ungodly technological advances, explored

161

the universe, cured diseases and we cultivated the world's greatest artists AND the world's greatest economy. We reached for the stars, acted like men. We aspired to intelligence, we didn't belittle it. It didn't make us feel inferior. We didn't identify ourselves by who we voted for in the last election and we didn't scare so easy. We were able to be all these things and do all these things because we were informed…by great men, men who were revered. First step in solving any problem is recognizing there is one. America is not the greatest country in the world anymore."

—Aaron Sorkin, *The Newsroom Script: Episode 1*

As the 44th President pointed out, it is now statistically harder to "make it" as a hardworking American than it is for those living within the national borders of virtually any of our wealthy allies. And it's our commitment to economic inequality that has gotten us there.

In this book, we explored how our education system is putting our public school kids behind in relation to other children around the world, building further debt into our middle class, and leading to a workforce that is woefully unprepared for the needs of twenty-first-century businesses.

How universal health care, which is available in every other modern nation and could *save* us taxpayer dollars, can't get implemented here because an oligopoly has their thumb on the left and right side of our Congress, keeping their pockets ever-wealthier as they profit off of a status quo that hurts everyone else.

How the middle class is, unequivocally, disappearing because the burdens of an unfair system are being placed on them. And, their political voice is being taken away from them by allowing elections to be won and lost by corporate sponsors. Replaced by an ever worse wake of immoral and partisan leaders.

How the news, which used to keep us informed, is now forced to care more about eyeballs than issues, because it's no longer a public good, but a for-profit business.

How we lead the world in incarceration, use our imprisoned labor in a way that amounts to a modern version of slavery, and yet, even with this mass incarceration, we have lost the war on drugs. In fact, today it's only marginally harder for youth to access drugs than alcohol. And as times get financially tougher, more people will resort to the escape offered via addiction—as we see evidenced in the growing opioid epidemic.

How we used to provide moral leadership in the world, but today we run from issues like clean energy and the environment. We leave our world weaker and lose out on the jobs of the future. Why? Because there is too much concentrated, economic power behind traditional industries that can readily guide our elected leaders to put their profit over the people of this country.

How it is a fact that many of us blame immigrants and globalization for our economic problems, but really we're just looking for a real path for the economic futures of our families. For stability. In fact, contrary to what many politicians would have us believe, immigrants contribute greatly to new companies, jobs, and prosperity in our country, and they always have. The problem is our elected leaders and their economic plan, not those who seek to become our fellow citizens.

How, across virtually every meaningful metric, we are way outside the red line of economic historical precedents, due to spiraling inequality. We are about to become the first generation in American history to be worse off than our parents.

How life has actually gotten harder for almost all of us. The youth among us just wanting the same shot Americans had twenty and thirty years ago, but changes in our system of government have made that dream slowly disappear.

But we have also discussed the fact that there is hope.

There is hope for change, and for improving our system of government and our society as a whole, if we unite ourselves and our voices in demanding it. We aren't Republicans. We aren't Democrats. We're Americans whose real enemy isn't *the other side*, but leadership *on both sides*.

Twilight of the Idols

The first step is recognizing that something fundamental has changed. Many of the ideals that have defined our country as one of the greatest the world has ever known have changed. If we fully embrace this reality, that we are not alone in the nagging feeling of doubt when we hear our leaders tell us that everyone is doing better than they ever have, then we can do something about it.

It's time to add a new chapter, a new ideal, to the American Dream. Rather than accepting a steady decline, we can do what our country was created to do, and truly allow the voice of the people to re-define our government. You are not powerless.

Again, let that sink in, because it's true: You are not powerless.

Together, we really can close the final chapter of money defining who gets elected, and being governed by politicians who've forgotten what it is to be anything else. If we can get our government back, then we can be the generation that proves, in the words of Lincoln, a government of the people, by the people, and for the people shall not perish from the earth.

Bibliography

"The 115th Congress Is among the Oldest in History." Quorum. Accessed December 2, 2018. https://www.quorum.us/data-driven-insights/the-115th-congress-is-among-the-oldest-in-history/175/.

"About Us: The Patriotic Millionaires." Patriotic Millionaires. Accessed November 27, 2018. https://patrioticmillionaires.org/about/.

Abramowicz, Lisa. "A Synthetic CDO by Any Other Name Is Still Risky." Bloomberg. Last modified February 3, 2017. https://www.bloomberg.com/gadfly/articles/2017-02-03/a-synthetic-cdo-by-any-other-name-is-still-risky.

Abramsky, Sasha. "Toxic Persons: New Research Shows Precisely How the Prison-to-Poverty Cycle Does Its Damage." *Slate Magazine.* Last modified October 8, 2010. http://www.slate.com/articles/news_and_politics/jurisprudence/2010/10/toxic_persons.html.

Alexander, Michelle. *The New Jim Crow: Mass Incarceration in the Age of Colorblindness.* New York: New Press, 2010.

Amadeo, Kimberly. "US GDP by Year Compared to Recessions and Events." The Balance. Last modified October 23, 2018. https://www.thebalance.com/us-gdp-by-year-3305543.

"America Might See a New Constitutional Convention in a Few Years." *The Economist.* Last modified September 30, 2017. https://www.economist.com/briefing/2017/09/30/america-might-see-a-new-constitutional-convention-in-a-few-years.

"The American Middle Class Is Losing Ground." Pew Research Center. Last modified December 9, 2015. http://www.pewsocialtrends.org/2015/12/09/the-american-middle-class-is-losing-ground/.

"The American Middle Class Loses Ground Nationally." Pew Research Center. Last modified May 11, 2016. http://www.pewsocialtrends.org/2016/05/11/1-the-american-middle-class-loses-ground-nationally/.

Andrlik, Todd. "How Old Were the Leaders of the American Revolution on July 4, 1776?" *Slate Magazine.* Last modified August 20, 2013. http://www.slate.com/articles/news_and_politics/politics/2013/08/how_old_were_the_founding_father_the_leaders_of_the_american_revolution.html.

Bibliography

Aubrey, Allison. "Whole Foods Says It Will Stop Selling Foods Made with Prison Labor." *NPR*. Last modified September 30, 2015. https://www.npr.org/sections/thesalt/2015/09/30/444797169/whole-foods-says-it-will-stop-selling-foods-made-by-prisoners

"Average (median) Household Income in the United States from 1990 to 2017 (in U.S. dollars)." Statista. Accessed November 26, 2018. https://www.statista.com/statistics/200838/median-household-income-in-the-united-states/.

Backman, Maurie. "This is the No. 1 Reason Americans File for Bankruptcy." The Motley Fool. Last modified May 1, 2017. https://www.fool.com/retirement/2017/05/01/this-is-the-no-1-reason-americans-file-for-bankrup.aspx.

Backman, Maurie. "Here's a Breakdown of the Average American's Household Debt." The Motley Fool. Last modified December 24, 2017. https://www.fool.com/retirement/2017/12/24/heres-a-breakdown-of-the-average-americans-househo.aspx.

Baicker, Katherine, David Cutler, and Zirui Song. "Workplace Wellness Programs Can Generate Savings." *Health Affairs* 29, no. 2 (2010). Last modified February 1, 2010. https://www.healthaffairs.org/doi/10.1377/hlthaff.2009.0626.

Banerjee, Abhijit V., Rema Hanna, Gabriel E. Kreindler, and Benjamin A. Olken. "Debunking the Stereotype of the Lazy Welfare Recipient: Evidence from Cash Transfer Programs." *The World Bank Research Observer* 32, no. 2 (2017): 155-184. Last modified August 30, 2017. https://academic.oup.com/wbro/article/32/2/155/4098285.

Barrett, Katherine and Richard Greene. "The Real Reason Behind Recent Teacher Strikes – and Why They're Likely to Continue." *Governing*. Last modified May 10, 2018. http://www.governing.com/topics/mgmt/gov-real-reason-teacher-strikes-continue.html.

Berezow, Alex. "Heroin Overdose Deaths Quadruple among Older Millennials." American Council on Science and Health. Last modified January 5, 2017. https://www.acsh.org/news/2017/01/05/heroin-overdose-deaths-quadruple-among-older-millennials-10690.

Berezow, Alex. "Only 6% of Americans Think the World Is Getting Better." American Council on Science and Health. Last modified July 3, 2016. https://www.acsh.org/news/2016/07/03/only-6-of-americans-think-world-is-getting-better.

Bibliography

Berezow, Alex and Brayden Olson. "Let Grad Students Teach Science to Kids: Column." *USA Today*. Last modified September 7, 2016. https://www.usatoday.com/story/opinion/2016/09/07/education-science-elementary-schools-graduate-students-teachers-column/89884940/.

Betancourt, Mark. "The Devastating Process of Dying in America without Insurance." *The Nation*. Last modified June 20, 2016. https://www.thenation.com/article/the-devastating-process-of-dying-in-america-without-insurance/.

Briana Boyington. "See 20 Years of Tuition Growth at National Universities." *U.S. News & World Report*. Accessed November 26, 2018. https://www.usnews.com/education/best-colleges/paying-for-college/articles/2017-09-20/see-20-years-of-tuition-growth-at-national-universities.

Brorsen, Les. "Looking behind the Declining Number of Public Companies." Harvard Law School. Last modified May 18, 2017. https://corpgov.law.harvard.edu/2017/05/18/looking-behind-the-declining-number-of-public-companies/.

Bryan, Bob. "There Are 9 Million More People Living in Poverty Now Than before the Great Recession." Business Insider. Last modified September 30, 2015. http://www.businessinsider.com/9-million-more-people-poverty-than-2007-2015-9.

Calfas, Jennifer. "Americans Have So Much Debt They're Taking It to The Grave." *Money*. Last modified March 22, 2017. http://time.com/money/4709270/americans-die-in-debt.

"Campaign Exposes Fissures over Issues, Values and How Life Has Changed in the U.S.," Pew Research Center. Last modified March 31, 2016. http://assets.pewresearch.org/wp-content/uploads/sites/5/2016/03/3-31-16-March-Political-release-1.pdf.

Chaudry, Ajay, Christopher Wimer, Suzanne Macartney, Lauren Frohlich, Colin Campbell, Kendall Swenson, Don Oellerich, and Susan Hauan. "Poverty in the United States: 50-Year Trends and Safety Net Impacts." U.S. Department of Health and Human Services. Last modified March 2016. https://aspe.hhs.gov/system/files/pdf/154286/50YearTrends.pdf.

Claxton, Gary, Bianca DiJulio, Heidi Whitmore, Jeremy D. Pickreign, Megan McHugh, Awo Osei-Anto, and Benjamin Finder. "Health Benefits in 2010: Premiums Rise Modestly, Workers Pay More toward Coverage." *Health Affairs* 29, no. 10 (2010). Last modified October 1, 2010. https://www.healthaffairs.org/doi/10.1377/hlthaff.2010.0725.

Bibliography

Collins, Chuck. "The Wealth of America's Three Richest Families Grew by 6,000% since 1982." *The Guardian*. Last modified October 31, 2018. https://www.theguardian.com/commentisfree/2018/oct/31/us-wealthiest-families-dynasties-governed-by-rich.

"Comptroller Stringer Report Finds Millennials Have Faced Toughest Economy since Great Depression." Office of the New York City Comptroller Scott M. Stringer Bureau of Budget. Last modified April 26, 2016. https://comptroller.nyc.gov/newsroom/comptroller-stringer-report-finds-millennials-have-faced-toughest-economy-since-great-depression/.

Cutler, David. "Why Does Health Care Cost So Much in America? Ask Harvard's David Cutler." PBS. Last modified November 19, 2013. https://www.pbs.org/newshour/economy/why-does-health-care-cost-so-m.

Delamaide, Darrell. "Opinion: The Democrats' 'Better Deal' Is a Box-Office Dud." MarketWatch. Last modified July 25, 2017. https://www.marketwatch.com/story/the-democrats-better-deal-is-a-box-office-dud-2017-07-25.

DeMichele, Thomas. "The U.S. Is the Only Very Highly Developed Country without Universal HealthCare." Fact / Myth. Last modified March 13, 2018. http://factmyth.com/factoids/the-us-is-the-only-very-highly-developed-country-without-universal-healthcare/.

DeSilver, Drew. "For Most U.S. Workers, Real Wages Have Barely Budged in Decades." Pew Research Center. Last Modified August 7, 2018. http://www.pewresearch.org/fact-tank/2018/08/07/for-most-us-workers-real-wages-have-barely-budged-for-decades/.

DeSilver, Drew. "U.S. Students' Academic Achievement Still Lags That of Their Peers in Many Other Countries." Pew Research Center. Last modified February 15, 2017. http://www.pewresearch.org/fact-tank/2017/02/15/u-s-students-internationally-math-science/.

DeSilver, Drew and Patrick Van Kessel. "As More Money Flows into Campaigns, Americans Worry about Its Influence." Pew Research Center. Last modified December 7, 2015. http://www.pewresearch.org/fact-tank/2015/12/07/as-more-money-flows-into-campaigns-americans-worry-about-its-influence/.

"Economic History of the United Kingdom: 1900-1945." Wikipedia. Accessed November 29, 2018. https://en.wikipedia.org/wiki/Economic_history_of_the_United_Kingdom#1900-1945.

Bibliography

"Education at a Glance 2014: OECD Indicators." OECD Publishing. Accessed November 29, 2018. https://read.oecd-ilibrary.org/ education/education-at-a-glance-2014_eag-2014-en#page4.

Eisen, Lauren-Brooke and Inimai Chettiar. "39% of Prisoners Should Not Be in Prison." *Time Magazine.* Last modified December 9, 2016. http://time.com/4596081/incarceration-report/.

Elkins, Kathleen. "Here's How Much Money Americans Have in Their Savings Accounts." *CNBC.* Last modified September 13, 2017. https://www.cnbc.com/2017/09/13/how-much-americans-at-have-in-their-savings-accounts.html.

Elliott, Larry. "Richest 62 People as Wealthy as Half of World's Population, Says Oxfam." *The Guardian.* Last modified January 18, 2016. https://www.theguardian.com/business/2016/jan/18/richest-62-billionaires-wealthy-half-world-population-combined.

"EMCDDA report presents latest evidence on heroin-assisted treatment for hard-to-treat opioid users." European Monitoring Centre for Drugs and Drug Addiction. Last modified April 19, 2012. http://www.emcdda.europa.eu/news/2012_en

Erickson, Jennifer ed. "The Middle-Class Squeeze." Center for American Progress. Last modified September 24, 2014. https://www.americanprogress.org/issues/economy/ reports/2014/09/24/96903/the-middle-class-squeeze/.

"The Fading American Dream." Opportunity Insights. Accessed December 2, 2018. https://opportunityinsights.org/.

Finnie, Hannah and Simran Jagtiani. "Millennials Crave Economic Stability and Opportunity." Generation Progress. Last modified September 2018. http://genprogress.org/wp-content/ uploads/2016/09/13114633/Millennials-Crave-Economic-Stability-And-Opportunity-Sept-2016.pdf.

Flock, Elizabeth. "APS (Atlanta Public Schools) Embroiled in Cheating Scandal." *The Washington Post.* Last modified July 2011. https:// www.washingtonpost.com/blogs/blogpost/post/aps-atlanta-public-schools-embroiled-in-cheating-scandal/2011/07/11/ gIQAJl9m8H_blog.html?utm_term=.6a28127a73fd.

Flounders, Sara. "The Pentagon and Slave Labor in U.S. Prisons." Global Research. Last modified September 1, 2018. http:// www.globalresearch.ca/the-pentagon-and-slave-labor-in-u-s-prisons/25376.

Bibliography

Fottrell, Quentin. "Millions of Americans Are One Pay Check Away from the Street." MarketWatch. Last modified January 20, 2018. https://www.marketwatch.com/story/most-americans-are-one-medical-emergency-away-from-financial-disaster-2017-01-12.

Fottrell, Quentin. "Most Americans Have Less Than $1,000 in Savings." MarketWatch. Last modified December 23, 2015. https://www.marketwatch.com/story/most-americans-have-less-than-1000-in-savings-2015-10-06.

"Four Pillars Drug Strategy." City of Vancouver. Accessed November 30, 2018. https://vancouver.ca/people-programs/four-pillars-drug-strategy.aspx.

Frank, Robert. "Did the Forbes 400 Billionaires Really 'Build That'?" CNBC. Last modified September 25, 2012. https://www.cnbc.com/id/49167533.

Frank, Robert. "The Stock Gap: American Stock Holdings at 18-Year Low." CNBC. Last modified September 4, 2014. https://www.cnbc.com/2014/09/08/the-stock-gap-american-stock-holdings-at-18-year-low.html.

Frey, Carl Benedikt, and Michael A. Osborne. "The Future of Employment: How Susceptible Are Jobs to Computerisation?" The Oxford Martin School at the University of Oxford. Last modified September 17, 2013. https://www.oxfordmartin.ox.ac.uk/downloads/academic/The_Future_of_Employment.pdf.

Fry, Richard. "It's Becoming More Common for Young Adults to Live at Home – and for Longer Stretches." Pew Research Center. Last modified May 5, 2017. http://www.pewresearch.org/fact-tank/2017/05/05/its-becoming-more-common-for-young-adults-to-live-at-home-and-for-longer-stretches/.

Fry, Richard and Rakesh Kochhar. "The Shrinking Middle Class in U.S. Metropolitan Areas: 6 Key Findings." Pew Research Center. Last modified May 12, 2016. http://www.pewresearch.org/fact-tank/2016/05/12/us-middle-class-metros-takeaways/.

Fry, Richard, Ruth Igielnik, and Eileen Patten. "How Millennials Today Compare with Their Grandparents 50 Years Ago." Pew Research Center. Last modified March 16, 2018. http://www.pewresearch.org/fact-tank/2018/03/16/how-millennials-compare-with-their-grandparents/.

Gandel, Stephen. "OMG, Young Millennials Are the Job Market's Biggest Losers." Fortune. Last modified March 4, 2016. http://fortune.com/2016/03/04/young-millennials-job-market-losers/.

Bibliography

Garofalo, Pat. "Romney: Students Should Get 'As Much Education as They Can Afford.'" Think Progress. Last modified June 29, 2012. https://thinkprogress.org/romney-students-should-get-as-much-education-as-they-can-afford-2b9f1275b85b/.

"Global Inequality." Inequality.org. Accessed November 29, 2018. https://inequality.org/facts/global-inequality/.

Glueck, Katie. "Poll: 75 Percent Want Hill Term Limits." *The Politico.* Last modified January 18, 2013. https://www.politico.com/story/2013/01/poll-75-percent-want-hill-term-limits-086378.

Glum, Julia. "53% of Millennials Expect to Become Millionaires One Day, according to a New Study." *Time Magazine.* Last modified June 11, 2018. http://time.com/money/5308043/millennials-millionaires-new-research/.

Gongloff, Mark. "45 Million Americans Still Stuck below Poverty Line: Census." *Huffington Post.* Last modified November 8, 2017. https://www.huffingtonpost.com/2014/09/16/poverty-household-income_n_5828974.html.

Gramlich, John. "America's Incarceration Rate Is at a Two-Decade Low." Pew Research Center. Last modified May 2, 2018. http://www.pewresearch.org/fact-tank/2018/05/02/americas-incarceration-rate-is-at-a-two-decade-low/.

Green, Bill. "Millennial Entrepreneurs Are Held Back Because of This 1 Reason." *Inc.* Last modified February 6, 2018. https://www.inc.com/bill-green/whats-holding-back-todays-millennial-entrepreneurs-and-what-they-need-to-succeed.html.

Gutscher, Cecile. "Subprime Auto Debt is Booming Even as Defaults Soar." Bloomberg. Last modified February 1, 2018. https://www.bloomberg.com/news/articles/2018-02-02/never-mind-defaults-debt-backed-by-subprime-auto-loans-is-hot.

Hamel, Liz, Mira Norton, Karen Pollitz, Larry Levitt, Gary Claxton, and Mollyann Brodie. "The Burden of Medical Debt: Results from the Kaiser Family Foundation/New York Times Medical Bills Survey." Kaiser Family Foundation. Last modified January 5, 2016. https://www.kff.org/report-section/the-burden-of-medical-debt-section-3-consequences-of-medical-bill-problems/.

Hargreaves, Steve. "Rich, Really Rich, and Ultra Rich." *CNN Business.* Last modified June 3, 2014. https://money.cnn.com/2014/06/01/luxury/rich-wealth-gap/index.html.

Bibliography

Hawkings, David. "Wealth of Congress: Richer than Ever, but Mostly at the Very Top." *Roll Call.* Last modified February 27, 2018. https://www.rollcall.com/news/hawkings/congress-richer-ever-mostly-top.

Hellmann, Jessie. "CBO: 18 Million Could Lose Coverage after ObamaCare Repeal." *The Hill.* Last modified January 17, 2017. http://thehill.com/policy/healthcare/314549-study-obamacare-repeal-could-leave-32-million-without-coverage.

Hensel, Daniel. "New Poll Shows Money in Politics Is a Top Voting Concern." Issue One. Last modified June 29, 2016. https://www.issueone.org/new-poll-shows-money-in-politics-is-a-top-voting-concern/.

Hirschler, Ben. "How the U.S. Pays 3 times More for Drugs." *Scientific American.* Accessed November 29, 2018. https://www.scientificamerican.com/article/how-the-u-s-pays-3-times-more-for-drugs/.

"HS393 Seed Enterprise Investment Scheme - Income Tax and Capital Gains Tax Reliefs (2017)." GOV.UK. Last modified April 9, 2018. https://www.gov.uk/government/publications/seed-enterprise-investment-scheme-income-tax-and-capital-gains-tax-reliefs-hs393-self-assessment-helpsheet/hs393-seed-enterprise-investment-scheme-income-tax-and-capital-gains-tax-reliefs-2017.

"Income Inequality in the United States." Inequality.org. Accessed November 29, 2018. https://inequality.org/facts/income-inequality/.

Ingraham, Christopher. "Massive New Data Set Suggests Economic Inequality is About to Get Even Worse." *The Washington Post.* Last modified January 10, 2018. https://www.washingtonpost.com/news/wonk/wp/2018/01/04/massive-new-data-set-suggests-inequality-is-about-to-get-even-worse/?utm_term=.a3713a891bbd.

Ingraham, Christopher. "The Richest 1 Percent Now Owns More of the Country's Wealth Than at Any Time in the Past 50 Years." *The Washington Post.* Last modified December 6, 2017. https://www.washingtonpost.com/news/wonk/wp/2017/12/06/the-richest-1-percent-now-owns-more-of-the-countrys-wealth-than-at-any-time-in-the-past-50-years/?utm_term=.9887fc21b26d.

Bibliography

Jones, Bradley. "Americans' Views of Immigrants Marked by Widening Partisan, Generational Divides." Pew Research Center. Last modified April 15, 2016. http://www.pewresearch.org/fact-tank/2016/04/15/americans-views-of-immigrants-marked-by-widening-partisan-generational-divides/.

Jones, Bradley. "Most Americans Want to Limit Campaign Spending, Say Big Donors Have Greater Political Influence." Pew Research Center. Last modified May 8, 2018. http://www.pewresearch.org/fact-tank/2018/05/08/most-americans-want-to-limit-campaign-spending-say-big-donors-have-greater-political-influence/.

"Just 8 Men Own Same Wealth as Half the World." Oxfam International. Last modified January 16, 2017. https://www.oxfam.org/en/pressroom/pressreleases/2017-01-16/just-8-men-own-same-wealth-half-world.

Kasperkevic, Jana. "Walmart Workers Increasingly Rely on Food Banks, Report Says." *The Guardian*. Last modified November 21, 2014. https://www.theguardian.com/money/us-money-blog/2014/nov/21/walmart-workers-rely-on-food-banks-report.

Katz, Lawrence F. and Alan B. Krueger. "Documenting Decline in U.S. Economic Mobility." *Science*. Last modified April 24, 2017. http://science.sciencemag.org/content/early/2017/04/21/science.aan3264.full.

Kelly, David. "Study Shows Employees Learn Best from Video Games." University of Colorado Denver. Last modified October 19, 2010. https://www.cudenvertoday.org/videogamesmakebetteremployees/.

Khullar, Dhruv. "As a Doctor, I See How a Lack of Health Insurance Worsens Illness and Suffering." *The Washington Post*. Last modified January 9, 2017. https://www.washingtonpost.com/news/to-your-health/wp/2017/01/09/doctors-see-how-a-lack-of-health-insurance-exacerbates-illness-and-suffering/?utm_term=.73c5731b0e5b.

Kochhar, Rakesh. "Are You in the Global Middle Class? Find Out with Our Income Calculator." Pew Research Center. Last modified July 16, 2016. http://www.pewresearch.org/fact-tank/2015/07/16/are-you-in-the-global-middle-class-find-out-with-our-income-calculator/.

Koepsell, David. "The Twilight of the Superhero." *International Policy Digest*. Last modified August 29, 2015. https://intpolicydigest. org/2015/08/29/the-twilight-of-the-superhero/.

Kondik, Kyle, and Geoffrey Skelley. "Incumbent Reelection Rates Higher than Average in 2016." University of Virginia Center for Politics. Last modified December 15th, 2016. http://www. centerforpolitics.org/crystalball/articles/incumbent-reelection-rates-higher-than-average-in-2016/.

Kopf, Dan. "The US Has More Immigrant Inventors Than Every Other Country Combined." Quartz. Last modified January 24, 2017. https://qz.com/890943/the-us-has-more-immigrant-inventors-than-every-other-country-combined/.

Kroll, Luisa. "The Forbes 400: The Richest People in America." *Forbes*. Last modified September 19, 2012. https://www.forbes.com/sites/luisakroll/2012/09/19/the-forbes-400-the-richest-people-in-america/#c749f9f4fd26.

Lane, April. "Beyond the Headlines: Is Student Debt Strangling Millennials' Chances for Success?" Bentley University. Accessed December 2, 2018. https://www.bentley.edu/impact/articles/beyond-headlines-student-debt-strangling-millennials-chances-success.

Law, Victoria. "Martori Farms: Abusive Conditions at a Key Wal-Mart Supplier." Truthout. Last modified June 24, 2011. https://truthout. org/articles/martori-farms-abusive-conditions-at-a-key-walmart-supplier/.

Layton, Lyndsey. "Study Says Standardized Testing Is Overwhelming Nation's Public Schools." *The Washington Post*. Last modified October 24, 2015. https://www.washingtonpost.com/local/education/study-says-standardized-testing-is-overwhelming-nations-public-schools/2015/10/24/8a22092c-79ae-11e5-a958-d889faf561dc_story.html?utm_term=.3e927ec25e80.

Leonhardt, David, and Kevin Quealy. "The American Middle Class Is No Longer the World's Richest." *The New York Times*. Last modified April 22, 2014. https://www.nytimes.com/2014/04/23/upshot/the-american-middle-class-is-no-longer-the-worlds-richest.html.

Leonhardt, Megan. "Millennials Ages 25–34 Have $42,000 in Debt, and Most of It Isn't from Student Loans." *CNBC*. Last modified August 16, 2018. https://www.cnbc.com/2018/08/15/millennials-have-42000-in-debt.html.

Bibliography

Levine, Peter. "The Waning Influence of American Political Parties." The Conversation. Last modified March 31, 2016. https://theconversation.com/the-waning-influence-of-american-political-parties-56875.

Lohr, Steve. "A.I. Is Doing Legal Work. But It Won't Replace Lawyers, Yet." *The New York Times*. Last modified March 19, 2017. https://www.nytimes.com/2017/03/19/technology/lawyers-artificial-intelligence.html.

"A Look at the Shocking Student Loan Debt Statistics for 2018." Student Loan Hero. Last modified May 1, 2018. https://studentloanhero.com/student-loan-debt-statistics/.

Lowery, Wesley. "91% of the Time the Better-Financed Candidate Wins. Don't Act Surprised." *The Washington Post*. Last modified April 4, 2014. https://www.washingtonpost.com/news/the-fix/wp/2014/04/04/think-money-doesnt-matter-in-elections-this-chart-says-youre-wrong/.

Luhby, Tami. "The 62 Richest People Have as Much Wealth as Half the World." *CNN Business*. Last modified January 18, 2016. http://money.cnn.com/2016/01/17/news/economy/oxfam-wealth/index.html?sr=twmoney011816oxfam-wealth0742AMStoryLink&linkId=20440984.

Mangan, Dan. "Medical Bills Are the Biggest Cause of US Bankruptcies: Study." *CNBC*. Last modified July 24, 2013. https://www.cnbc.com/id/100840148 .

Martin, Emmie. "Here's How Much the Average American Earns at Every Age." *CNBC*. Last modified August 24, 2017. https://www.cnbc.com/2017/08/24/how-much-americans-earn-at-every-age.html.

McArdle, Megan. "The Truth about Medical Bankruptcies." *The Washington Post*. Last modified March 26, 2018. https://www.washingtonpost.com/blogs/post-partisan/wp/2018/03/26/the-truth-about-medical-bankruptcies/?utm_term=.b6f31fae1207.

McKenzie, Brian. "Who Drives to Work? Commuting by Automobile in the United States: 2013." United States Census Bureau. Last modified August 2015. https://www.census.gov/content/dam/Census/library/publications/2015/acs/acs-32.pdf.

McLaughlin, John and Brittany Davin. "M&A Poll: Voters Overwhelmingly Support Term Limits for Congress." McLaughlin & Assoc. Accessed November 26, 2018. http://mclaughlinonline.com/2018/02/08/ma-poll-voters-overwhelmingly-support-term-limits-for-congress/.

Bibliography

McPhillips, Deidre. "Quality of Life Rankings." *U.S. News & World Report.* Last modified January 23, 2018. https://www.usnews.com/news/best-countries/quality-of-life-full-list.

"Median and Average Sale Price of Houses Sold in the United States." United States Census Bureau. Accessed November 26, 2018. https://www.census.gov/construction/nrs/pdf/uspricemon.pdf.

"The Millennial Generation Research Review." U.S. Chamber of Commerce Foundation. Last modified November 12, 2012. https://www.uschamberfoundation.org/reports/millennial-generation-research-review.

Monahan, Kelly, Jeff Schwartz, and Tiffany Schleeter. "Decoding Millennials in the Gig Economy." Deloitte Insights. Last modified May 1, 2018. https://www2.deloitte.com/insights/us/en/focus/technology-and-the-future-of-work/millennials-in-the-gig-economy.html.

Money Still Wins 91% of Congressional Races, 2014. Represent.us. http://bulletin.represent.us/wp-content/uploads/sites/3/2015/10/MoneyWinsCongress14_C.gif.

Money Wins Congressional Races 91% of the Time, 2012. Represent.us. https://visual.ly/community/infographic/politics/how-money-won-congress.

Mudede, Charles. "Why It's Misleading to Say the 62 Richest People Have the Same Wealth as Half the World." *The Stranger.* Last modified January 18, 2016. https://www.thestranger.com/blogs/slog/2016/01/18/23441405/why-its-misleading-to-say-the-62-richest-people-have-the-same-wealth-as-half-the-world.

Natarajan, Sridhar, Dakin Campbell, and Alastair Marsh. "Citi Is Bringing Back One of the Most Infamous Bets of the Credit Crisis." Bloomberg. Last modified September 26, 2017. https://www.bloomberg.com/news/articles/2017-09-26/as-synthetic-cdos-roar-back-a-young-citi-trader-makes-her-name.

Nikiforos, Michalis, Marshall Steinbaum, and Gennaro Zezza. "Modeling the Macroeconomic Effects of a Universal Basic Income." Roosevelt Institute. Last modified August 8, 2017. http://rooseveltinstitute.org/modeling-macroeconomic-effects-ubi/.

"Offenses." Federal Bureau of Prisons. Last modified October 27, 2018. https://www.bop.gov/about/statistics/statistics_inmate_offenses.jsp.

Bibliography

Pearson, Natalie Obiko. "Vancouver's Hot Housing Market Gets Tougher for Wealthy Chinese." Bloomberg. Last modified February 20, 2018. https://www.bloomberg.com/news/articles/2018-02-20/british-columbia-extends-housing-crackdown-with-tax-increases.

Phillips, Matt. "Chinese Money is Pouring into Seattle and Making Homes Crazy Expensive." *Vice News.* Last modified February 9, 2017. *https://*news.vice.com/en_us/article/j5d7e4/chinese-money-is-pouring-into-seattle-and-making-homes-crazy-expensive.

"Physician Study: Quantifying the Cost of Defensive Medicine." Jackson Healthcare. Last modified February 2010. https://jacksonhealthcare.com/media-room/surveys/defensive-medicine-study-2010/.

"Poverty rate in the United States from 1990 to 2017." Statista. Accessed November 26, 2018. https://www.statista.com/statistics/200463/us-poverty-rate-since-1990/.

Powell, Benjamin. "The Economics behind the U.S. Government's Unwinnable War on Drugs." The Library of Economics and Liberty. Last modified July 1, 2013. http://www.econlib.org/library/Columns/y2013/Powelldrugs.html.

"The Productivity–Pay Gap." Economic Policy Institute. Last modified August 2018. https://www.epi.org/productivity-pay-gap/.

"The Proposals." A Better Deal. Accessed December 2, 2018. https://abetterdeal.democraticleader.gov/category/the-proposals/.

"Public Opinion on Civil Rights: Reflections on the Civil Rights Act of 1964." Roper Center for Public Opinion Research. Accessed December 2, 2018. https://ropercenter.cornell.edu/public-opinion-on-civil-rights-reflections-on-the-civil-rights-act-of-1964/.

"Public Trust in Government: 1958–2017." Pew Research Center. Last modified December 14, 2017. http://www.people-press.org/2017/12/14/public-trust-in-government-1958-2017/.

Rabuy, Bernadette and Daniel Kopf. "Prisons of Poverty: Uncovering the Pre-incarceration Incomes of the Imprisoned." Prison Policy Initiative. Last modified July 9, 2015. https://www.prisonpolicy.org/reports/income.html.

"Remarks by the President on Economic Mobility." The White House: President Barack Obama. Last modified December 4, 2013. https://obamawhitehouse.archives.gov/the-press-office/2013/12/04/remarks-president-economic-mobility.

Bibliography

"Report on the Economic Well-Being of U.S. Households in 2015." Board of Governors of the Federal Reserve System. Last modified May 2016. https://www.federalreserve.gov/2015-report-economic-well-being-us-households-201605.pdf.

Riffkin, Rebecca. "Public Faith in Congress Falls Again, Hits Historic Low." Gallup. Last modified June 19, 2014. http://news.gallup.com/poll/171710/public-faith-congress-falls-again-hits-historic-low.aspx.

"The Rise in Dual Income Households." Pew Research Center. Last modified June 18, 2015. http://www.pewresearch.org/ft_dual-income-households-1960-2012-2/.

Ritholtz, Barry. "Where Have All the Public Companies Gone?" Bloomberg. Last modified June 24, 2015. https://www.bloomberg.com/view/articles/2015-06-24/where-have-all-the-publicly-traded-companies-gone-.

Roberts, Jeff J. "7 Well-Known Tech Firms Founded by Immigrants or Their Children." *Fortune.* Last modified January 30, 2017. http://fortune.com/2017/01/30/tech-immigrant-founders/.

Rosenberg, Mike. "Nearly Half of Local Millennials Consider Moving as Seattle-Area Home Costs Soar Again." *The Seattle Times.* Last modified February 28, 2017. https://www.seattletimes.com/business/real-estate/nearly-half-of-local-millennials-consider-moving-as-seattle-area-home-costs-soar-again/.

Rothwell, Jonathan. "How the War on Drugs Damages Black Social Mobility." Brookings. Last modified September 30, 2014. https://www.brookings.edu/blog/social-mobility-memos/2014/09/30/how-the-war-on-drugs-damages-black-social-mobility/.

Rotman, David. "How Technology Is Destroying Jobs." *MIT Technology Review.* Last modified June 12, 2013. https://www.technologyreview.com/s/515926/how-technology-is-destroying-jobs/.

Rugaber, Christopher S. "Pay Gap between College Grads and Everyone Else at a Record." *USA Today.* Last modified January 12, 2017. https://www.usatoday.com/story/money/2017/01/12/pay-gap-between-college-grads-and-everyone-else-record/96493348/.

Saez, Emmanuel. "Striking it Richer: The Evolution of Top Incomes in the United States (Updated with 2015 preliminary estimates)." Econometrics Laboratory at the University of California at Berkeley. Last modified June 30, 2016. https://eml.berkeley.edu/~saez/saez-UStopincomes-2015.pdf.

Bibliography

Saez, Emmanuel and Gabriel Zucman. "Exploding Wealth Inequality in the United States." Washington Center for Equitable Growth. Last modified October 20, 2014. https://equitablegrowth.org/exploding-wealth-inequality-united-states.

Schoen, John W. "Study: 1.2 Million Households Lost to Recession." *NBC News.* Last modified April 8, 2010. http://www.nbcnews.com/id/36231884/ns/business-eye_on_the_economy/t/study-million-households-lost-recession/.

Semuels, Alana. "New Census Data Shows More Americans Emerging from Poverty." *The Atlantic.* Last modified September 12, 2017. https://www.theatlantic.com/business/archive/2017/09/new-census-data-shows-more-americans-emerging-from-poverty/539589/.

Sered, Susan. "Uninsured Americans Tell Their Stories." The Commonwealth Fund. Accessed November 29, 2018. https://www.commonwealthfund.org/publications/publication/uninsured-americans-tell-their-stories.

Sheng, Ellen. "Seattle Real Estate Sees Surge in Chinese Interest after Vancouver Enacts 15% Tax." *Forbes.* Last modified March 2, 2017. https://www.forbes.com/sites/ellensheng/2017/03/02/seattle-real-estate-sees-surge-in-chinese-interest-after-vancouver-enacts-15-tax/#35c51f8a65e1.

"Small Business Venture Capital Tax Credit." Government of British Columbia. Accessed December 2, 2018. https://www2.gov.bc.ca/gov/content/taxes/income-taxes/corporate/credits/venture-capital.

Smith, Samantha. "Why People Are Rich and Poor: Republicans and Democrats Have Very Different Views." Pew Research Center. Last modified May 2, 2017. http://www.pewresearch.org/fact-tank/2017/05/02/why-people-are-rich-and-poor-republicans-and-democrats-have-very-different-views/

Straubhaar, Thomas. "On the Economics of a Universal Basic Income." *Intereconomics* 52, no. 2 (2017): 74-80. Accessed November 29, 2018. https://archive.intereconomics.eu/year/2017/2/on-the-economics-of-a-universal-basic-income/.

Strauss, Valerie. "Report: Big Education Firms Spend Millions Lobbying for Pro-testing Policies." *The Washington Post.* Last modified March 30, 2015. https://www.washingtonpost.com/news/answer-sheet/wp/2015/03/30/report-big-education-firms-spend-millions-lobbying-for-pro-testing-policies/?utm_term=.dbe0938ff579.

Bibliography

"Sue-Happy America." eLocal Legal Resource Network. Last modified September 7, 2011. https://www.elocal.com/content/legal-resource-network/sue-happy-america-2115.

Szalavitz, Maia. "Addictions Are Harder to Kick When You're Poor. Here's Why." *The Guardian*. Last modified June 1, 2016. https://www.theguardian.com/commentisfree/2016/jun/01/drug-addiction-income-inequality-impacts-recovery.

Taber, Jennifer M., Bryan Leyva, and Alexander Persoskie. "Why Do People Avoid Medical Care? A Qualitative Study Using National Data." *Journal of General Internal Medicine* 30, no. 3 (2014): 290-7. Last modified November 12, 2014. https://www.ncbi.nlm.nih.gov/pmc/articles/PMC4351276/.

Takeo, Ryan. "$72,000 Considered 'Low Income' in King, Snohomish Counties for Family of Four." *King 5 News*. Last modified April 26, 2017. http://www.king5.com/article/news/local/72000-considered-low-income-in-king-snohomish-counties-for-family-of-four/281-434107397.

Tepper, Taylor. "Millennials in China are Twice as Likely to Own Homes as Young Americans." *Money*. Last modified April 10, 2017. http://time.com/money/4732889/millennials-home-ownership-china-america/.

Thoma, Mark. "Remarks by the President on Economic Mobility." *Economist's View*. Last modified December 4, 2013. https://economistsview.typepad.com/economistsview/2013/12/remarks-by-the-president-on-economic-mobility.html.

"Thomas Jefferson to Richard Price." Library of Congress. Accessed December 2, 2018. https://www.loc.gov/exhibits/jefferson/60.html.

Thompson, Derek. "The Myth of the Millennial Entrepreneur." *The Atlantic*. Last modified July 6, 2016. https://www.theatlantic.com/business/archive/2016/07/the-myth-of-the-millennial-entrepreneur/490058/.

"Transnational Institute Progress Report as a Contribution to the Mid-Term (2003) Review of UNGASS." Transnational Institute. Accessed November 30, 2018. https://www.tni.org/files/download/brief6.pdf.

"U.S. Constitution Threatened as Article V Convention Movement Nears Success." Common Cause. Last modified September 2018. https://www.commoncause.org/wp-content/uploads/2018/09/Article-V-Memo-Sept-2018.pdf.

Bibliography

"U.S. Population." Worldometers. Accessed December 2, 2018. http://www.worldometers.info/world-population/us-population/.

"U.S. Prison Population Declined One Percent in 2014." Bureau of Justice Statistics. last modified September 17, 2015. https://www.bjs.gov/content/pub/press/p14pr.cfm.

Villacorta, Natalie. "Poll: Half of Millennials Independent." *The Politico*. Last modified March 7, 2014. https://www.politico.com/story/2014/03/millennials-independence-poll-104401.

Weissman, Jordan. "Think We're the Most Entrepreneurial Country in the World? Not So Fast." *The Atlantic*. Last modified October 2, 2012. https://www.theatlantic.com/business/archive/2012/10/think-were-the-most-entrepreneurial-country-in-the-world-not-so-fast/263102/.

West, Larry. "Global Warming to Cause Food Shortages." ThoughtCo. Last modified January 11, 2018. https://www.thoughtco.com/global-warning-to-cause-food-shortages-1203847.

"What Can History Teach Us about Technology and Jobs?" McKinsey Global Institute. Last modified February 2018. https://www.mckinsey.com/featured-insights/future-of-organizations-and-work/what-can-history-teach-us-about-technology-and-jobs.

White, Martha C. "Locked-In Profits: The U.S. Prison Industry, by the Numbers." *NBC News*. November 2, 2015. https://www.nbcnews.com/business/business-news/locked-in-profits-u-s-prison-industry-numbers-n455976.

Winick, Erin. "Lawyer-Bots Are Shaking Up Jobs." *MIT Technology Review*. Last modified December 12, 2017. https://www.technologyreview.com/s/609556/lawyer-bots-are-shaking-up-jobs/.

Winter, Caroline. "What Do Prisoners Make for Victoria's Secret?" *Mother Jones*. Last modified August 2008. https://www.motherjones.com/politics/2008/07/what-do-prisoners-make-victorias-secret/.

Witko, Christopher. "How Wall Street Became a Big Chunk of the U.S. Economy — and When the Democrats Signed On." *The Washington Post*. Last modified March 29, 2016. https://www.washingtonpost.com/news/monkey-cage/wp/2016/03/29/how-wall-street-became-a-big-chunk-of-the-u-s-economy-and-when-the-democrats-signed-on/?utm_term=.440e0068d946.

Bibliography

Wolff, Richard. "The Myth of 'American Exceptionalism' Implodes." *The Guardian.* Last modified January 18, 2011. https://www. theguardian.com/commentisfree/cifamerica/2011/jan/17/ economics-globalrecessionf.

"World Drug Report 2015." United Nations Office on Drugs and Crime. Accessed November 29, 2018. https://www.unodc.org/ documents/wdr2015/World_Drug_Report_2015.pdf.

"World Prison Populations." *BBC News.* Accessed November 29, 2018. http://news.bbc.co.uk/2/shared/spl/hi/uk/06/prisons/html/ nn2page1.stm.

Zambas, Joanna. "10 Companies That Use Prison Labour to Rake In Profits." Career Addict. Last modified October 11, 2017. https:// www.careeraddict.com/prison-labour-companies.

Zenger, Jack. "Great Leaders Can Double Profits, Research Shows." *Forbes.* Last modified January 15, 2015. https://www.forbes.com/ sites/jackzenger/2015/01/15/great-leaders-can-double-profits-research-shows/#26844ccf6ca6.

Brayden isn't your typical political author. As an inventor, his work became the recipient of a National Science Foundation grant for education technology now used by more than 50 universities. As an entrepreneur, he was selected as a Fortune magazine "Startup Idol" and is the youngest member ever admitted to the Seattle Entrepreneurs' organization. As a civic activist, his work and writing is fueled by firsthand experience growing up without resources, fighting for his American Dream, and then witnessing the political and economic changes that are closing that door on our next generation.

CPSIA information can be obtained
at www.ICGtesting.com
Printed in the USA
FSHW011826260519
58473FS